THE REINCARNATION
OF
JOHN WILKES BOOTH

The evil that men do lives after them,
The good is oft interred with their bones.

—SHAKESPEARE: *Julius Caesar*

THE REINCARNATION OF JOHN WILKES BOOTH

A Study in Hypnotic Regression
by
Dell Leonardi

The Devin-Adair Company
Old Greenwich, Connecticut

To my husband
Lenny

ISBN No. 0–8159–6716–0

Library of Congress Catalog No. 74–27952

Printed in the United States of America

PUBLISHER'S PREFACE

The manuscript of this astounding book came to us through a friend of many years, Arthur Sheehan: researcher and author.

Arthur told how an advertisement of his in the personal columns of the *Saturday Review,* offering his services in research, had brought a response from Dell Leonardi, Ph.D., of Kansas City, who wanted to verify certain sailing dates in the 1860s. Specifically, had there been a vessel with the name Margaret in it, whose master, a man named Henrichsen, sailed it from San Francisco to England in the winter of 1865–66?

Through the friendly cooperation of the people at Lloyds, who referred him to the Seamen's Church Institute in New York, it seemed that indeed there had been ten ships in the British merchant fleet of that day with Margaret as part of their name, including the *Margaret Kinch,* under the command of a Captain C. Henrichsen, which made a regular run from Liverpool to San Francisco in the 1860s.

That small happening, which could not possibly have been known to "Wesley," the young man who is the medium through whom Booth "reappears" in this book, persuaded the author—a professional hypnotist—to continue the hypnotic regressions that she had undertaken, and to dig further into the strange personality that emerged, purportedly as John Wilkes Booth, President Lincoln's assassin, whenever she regressed "Wesley."

Seventy-three hours of taped questions and answers, with her subject under hypnosis, resulted in the revelation of some extraordinary information: that arrangements had been made for Booth's escape, and for a stand-in, or double, to take his place; that he had managed to make his way to San Francisco whence he set sail for England; that, under a new name, he subsequently become a noted actor in England, and that he died in Calais, France.

Being somewhat skeptical—as well as fascinated—by the story, I took a plane to Kansas City to meet the author and her subject. On a Sunday evening, I watched her hypnotize "Wesley," observed him as he became "someone else," and listened to questions and answers for the better part of an hour. It was my impression that the performance was a genuine one; that Dell Leonardi was, and is, a person of integrity, and that her subject had no recollection of what went on during the session after he "came out." The fact that "Wesley" has no recollection whatsoever of the many hours of regression, seems reason enough to accord him the requested anonymity of his pseudonym. He is a young man in his early twenties with a farming background.

Was Booth the man who died on the porch at the Garrett farm? Students of history have asked this question, and it is shadowed by a darker question—was the murder and makeshift burial of a man thought to be Booth an elaborate cover up by Secretary of War Stanton because he had allowed the assassin of President Lincoln to *escape?*

It seems strange that the body of John Wilkes Booth, shrouded in canvas with a guncase for a coffin, was buried under the floor of the Old Penitentiary for four years, notwithstanding pleas by the Booth family to claim it. Equally strange was Stanton's cruel torture of the doomed conspirators, each shackled to a seventy-five-pound iron ball, his head encased in heavy canvas padded an inch thick with cotton, with one small hole for eating through, no opening for eyes or ears, and laced so tightly around the neck that he could not speak except at the trial when the hood was removed.

What separated those who were to be condemned at any cost from those about whose fate the War Department was indifferent? The government had a wide choice of victims who could have been charged with helping Booth, and had offered a reward of $100,000—$75,000 of it for the capture of the fugitives, Booth and Herold. Stanton had issued this declaration:

> All persons harboring or secreting the said persons, or either of them, or aiding or assisting their concealment or escape, will be treated as accomplices in the murder of the President and the attempted assassination of the Secretary of State, [Seward] and shall be subject to trial before a Military Commission and the punishment of DEATH.

Nothing could be more explicit, but the bureau of military justice was to divide its prisoners into two groups—treating one with extreme severity, and the other with extreme leniency—although this second group included such men as the three confederate soldiers who guided the fugitives to their hiding place at the Garrett farm.

It may be more than conjecture that powerful forces were behind a plan for Booth's escape—including the influential and secret organization known as the Knights of the Golden Circle. That government files do not always yield information on sensitive matters is not without precedent—nor is it without sequel in the 1970s. This was intimated by Donn Piatt, one of Stanton's friends, who reported to the War Minister after the conclusion of a trial at which he had served as judge advocate.

"Mr. Stanton," Judge Piatt wrote later, "examined me at length as to what had been proven, and I saw an expression very like heat-lightning flash over his face. . . . After the death of the secretary it was discovered that the entire record had disappeared."

Booth's diary was impounded by Stanton for two years after the assassination, and when it finally was released, eighteen pages were missing. It became known that Booth had not changed his plan from kidnapping to murder until the day of his crime, but much of what happened after the assassination has been clouded by conflicting testimony—by evidence and insinuation, truth, partial truth and government-inspired prejudice.

Many facts are known about the life of John Wilkes Booth, but mystery continues to surround the events leading to his death. Perhaps, in this account of hypnotic regression, Dell Leonardi has contributed a clue.

Whether Booth escaped alive, as some think, or was shot down in Garrett's barn, and whether Booth acted alone, or was associated with a group known as the Knights of the Golden Circle, makes for fascinating speculation. This book can only add to the lingering mystery.

Even more to the point, is "Wesley's" body a true receptacle for a reincarnated John Wilkes Booth? Let the reader be the judge.

—DEVIN A. GARRITY

CONTENTS

I hold that when a person dies,
His soul returns again to earth;
Arrayed in some new flesh-disguise
Another mother gives him birth.
With sturdier limbs and brighter brain
The old soul takes the road again.

—JOHN MASEFIELD

I have been here before,
But where or how I cannot tell;
I know the grass beyond the door,
The sweet, keen smell,
The sighing sound; the lights around the shore.
You have been mine before,
How long ago I may not know;
But just when at that swallow's soar
Your neck turned so,
Some veil did fall—I knew it all of yore.

—DANTE GABRIEL ROSSETTI

AUTHOR'S INTRODUCTION

IN RECENT YEARS OCCULT STUDIES HAVE TAKEN A GIANT step out of the superstitious shadows into the light of intellectual acceptance. In a letter dated July 24, 1921, Freud wrote to an English psychical searcher, Hereward Carrington: "I do not belong with those who reject in advance the study of so-called occult phenomena as being unscientific, or unworthy, or harmful. If I were at the beginning of my scientific career, instead of at the end of it as I am now, I might perhaps choose no other field of study—in spite of all its difficulties."

Hypnotism is a strange aspect of human consciousness, and an aura of mystery continues to cling to the ancient practice of the art. Born of the occult, cloaked in witchcraft and superstition, it remains to the present time repugnant to many. It has been lauded by charlatans as a panacea for almost all human suffering, but only recently has it been accepted as useful in the practice of medicine and dentistry.

11

For more than twenty years, hypnotism has been my familiar ground. Although my practice in hypnotherapy is limited to such things as smoking, weight control, insomnia, memory and other basic human problems, my real interest is much broader. I have found the work rewarding and fascinating. I have seen good results from the proper use of hypnotism, and although much is known, there is much to learn.

Witches at one time were burned or hanged. This practice is no longer acceptable, but man in his cultural advance has learned to crucify with words. If we do not want to be labeled "crack-pot," we must bring clear minds, not fantasies, to our research. We must bring proof, not superstition. We must open ourselves to controlled experimentation and not show bristling contempt when proof is demanded of us. We must stand proud in the light of criticism and have no fear of truth.

Occultism, at last, has a foot in the door of respectability, but we who are fighting to enter must remember that we are guests to a host of nonbelievers and must wipe the mud from our shoes before entering. A certain stigma is still attached to those who dare to delve into the supernatural and reach beyond the limits of ordinary religious concepts.

When Morey Bernstein, a Colorado businessman and admitted amateur in hypnotism, startled the country with his book, *The Search for Bridey Murphy,* many experts dismissed it as fantasy woven subconsciously by a young housewife who allegedly recalled a previous lifetime in Ireland. There were those, however, who believed in the Bernstein experiment, and all over America little living room games were going on. The game was regression, and the object was "Who could remember being someone else?"

Hypnotists soon found that there were limitations to these games. Few subjects could be prebirth regressed because most were incapable of the deep-trance states necessary for remembering past lives. In my own experience, I have found only ten per cent of those hypnotized able to arrive at this deep-trance state, or to remember anything beyond this lifetime. For the majority, hypnosis is merely a deeply relaxed condition with an awareness of surroundings—such as one experiences while watching television.

When I first met Wesley, I had almost lost hope of learning anything significant by experimenting with prebirth regression. Although I continued to regress suitable subjects as part of my class instruction, my classes were primarily intended for self-improvement, and for teaching self-hypnosis to students to help them overcome personality problems and utilize their minds to a greater extent. Wesley wanted to improve his study habits and had no knowledge of, nor prior experience with, hypnosis. He was nearly twenty-one when he enrolled in my class, and was friendly and outgoing, with the appearance of being older than his years. From the beginning it was evident that he was an excellent subject for hypnosis, and he allowed me to use him for various experiments.

As the class progressed, the subject of prebirth regression was presented. The students wondered if they might have a chance to witness this phenomenon, and because Wesley seemed to be the only student capable of such an undertaking, I asked his permission to try. Wesley laughed and said that, although he didn't believe in reincarnation and knew he had never lived before, he had no objection to my experimenting with him.

Let us consider some theories explaining reincarnation via hypnosis: One claims that the subject recalls bits and pieces of information stored in his subconscious mind, and under hypnosis is capable of building a subconscious fantasy. Another prevalent theory is that the subject will try to please the hypnotist; if he thinks that the hypnotist wants him to recall a previous life, he will accommodate. A third states that the subject may be able to draw knowledge from the mind of the hypnotist, and repeat information that the hypnotist has unwittingly supplied.

The last two theories lose credibility when they are explored logically, or as a challenge to the first theory. Why would a subject prefer to be a plain "Bridey Murphy," instead of "Joan of Arc," or "Cleopatra?" When one considers the amount of time spent learning facts surrounding famous lives, it would seem that the ego might attach itself more readily to these individuals than to some unknown identity such as "Bridey Murphy" or "Jane Doe."

No theory seemed to apply to the case of Wesley, and I had no criteria to follow, but this study in depth hypnosis is unique because the subject remembered the life that he had lived in a prior existence. Other investigations have lacked the vital fact of the subject's known identity. The hypnotist who is placed at this disadvantage has no way in which to unlock the stored memories of the subject.

The mind does not think of one thing at a time, but in a series or chain of thoughts. For example: one might think of a car, and what comes to mind? A certain color, model, and identity, the car that you own or would like to own, a friend's car, etc. Someone asks you, "Do you remember Tom Winters?" You immediately begin to search your mind for the name. If he adds, "You remember, he was the one who smoked the pipe," this information quickly helps you to identify a particular "Tom."

This applied to the experiment with Wesley, but because in his former life he had met thousands of people, his case was complicated by the double or triple life aspect. When I asked about a name, Wesley had to search for something to connect it to. Sometimes he was able to supply a reference that agreed with what I knew, but if not, I would have to accept what he said and hope that he had made the proper association.

My choice of words was important. Any psychologist knows that a patient is able to talk openly about his problem if the psychologist provides a soft pillow of understanding upon which he may safely unburden his troubles. One look of shock or word of condemnation from the psychologist, or a tone of voice that might suggest that what he is hearing contradicts his own moral concepts, and the patient will tighten up, causing the fragile rapport to be lost.

The early regressions in the Wesley study were disappointing. They were conducted once a week, and the questions and answers were taped. My recording equipment was poor and the microphones picked up outside noise that drifted in through the open windows. There was air conditioning, but we had to turn it off during the regressions or we could not have heard at all. If you have ever had occasion to be in the midwestern United States during the late spring or summer months, you can appreciate how we suffered. Our room was usually crowded with spectators who only added to the problem.

Many aspects of the regressions disturbed me, but I had to control my private feelings and present nothing but a quiet, compassionate voice leading Wesley back in time to relive and unravel the tangle of agonizing memories from his former life. I had one prime question to ask, after I had taken him beyond his own lifetime, and his answer carried me over the threshold into a strange new adventure that was to absorb my mind, my energy and my emotions for many months to come.

Q. You are now somewhere in the 1800s. What is your full name?

15

There was no sound in the room except for the noise of traffic drifting in through the open window. Every eye was fixed upon the still face of Wesley as his lips slowly formed the words, and in a strange, soft voice he replied.

A. My name is . . . John Wilkes Booth.

1
THE MYSTERY BEGINS

I HAVE TALKED WITH THE INFAMOUS JOHN WILKES BOOTH.
I believe that to be a fact.

For many months, the young man whom I know as
Wesley visited my home and allowed himself to be prebirth regressed. Every Sunday night, for three years, he
came to seat himself in a comfortable chair in my living
room, knowing that there would be microphones posi-
tioned directly over his head.

A selected group of spectators from my classes were
invited, and by eight-thirty all had found seats. The po-
lite conversation faded to whispers, and the lights were
lowered as we sat in silence.

I offered a prayer before speaking the words that
would open the doors of Wesley's mind to the 1800s. His
familiar form was at ease as I ended my hypnotic intro-
duction with these words:

"You are now able to see your life as John Wilkes
Booth. You have nothing to fear, and you can talk to me

openly and honestly about events when I ask you questions."

At the sound of my words, Wesley slowly lifted his head and pulled his body upright. The facial expression had changed. It was as though he had somehow slipped out of his body, and in his place sat the now familiar actor. His rich, full voice tinged with a British accent, firmly answered my questions.

As he recounted the assassination of Abraham Lincoln, the wounds that had been healed by time suddenly became raw. The assassin relived the moment of his crime, and then step by agonizing step, retraced his journey from Washington to the Garrett farm; from there to San Francisco, and eventually to England. He related the elaborate plan of escape mapped by one of the largest organizations of treason the world has ever known, The Knights of the Golden Circle.

Booth told of the unfortunate man who met his end at the Garrett farm and spoke of his friend, Davy Herold, who blundered and was captured there.

The impossible idea of an actor, dead for almost a century, stepping from the wings of eternity to appear in the 1970s for a final "curtain call," may cause many to scoff, but I am certain that there will be believers in the audience.

Looking back on my own thoughts that first night, it seems to me that they were no different from other cases where I had placed a subject under hypnosis for the purpose of regression. There were the usual apprehensions because the regressive states include dangers not present in ordinary applications of hypnosis. Because I am aware of these dangers, I admit that I am not as relaxed and confident while working with a prebirth regression as I am with other phases of hypnotism. The hypnotist working in any area of age regression risks arousing the highly traumatic incidents of our lives which lie buried in the subconscious. When these semidormant memories are stirred by hypnosis, the memory comes to life as vividly as if the incident had just occurred. Before an attempt is made to uncover a previous lifetime, it is necessary to cause the subject to relive memories from earlier years of his present life.

The hypnotist has to use tact while regressing a subject before an audience. Although it is unlikely that a hypnotized person will reveal any private incident before a group (in his adult mind), he might recall an incident from early childhood and, in the regressed mind of a child, blurt out something that could cause embarrassment later. One way to avoid this is to take the subject back to his childhood memories of Christmas or a birthday. One may hope that these special days were pleasant for him.

Wesley was seated in a comfortable chair, with the tape recorder turned on. The lights were lowered and there was silence as I eased him back into time by suggesting that each number was his age. I began the count at twenty, his age at the time; counted backward, nineteen, eighteen, seventeen. . . . I stopped at the count of five. The regression from the tapes follows:

Q. You are now five years old. How old are you, Wesley?
A. *(childish voice)* Five.
Q. All right, I am going to continue to count backward; each number is to be your age. Four, three, two, one. You are now one-year old and growing even younger, we are now at the moment of your birth and we are still moving backward, further and further back, moving out into space, and I want you to continue to go back in time until you see something *(letting him drift a moment)*. Tell me, what do you see?
A. Light.
Q. Where are you?
A. Maryland.

19

Q. What is the year?
A. 1863.
Q. What is your name?
A. John.
Q. What is your last name?
A. Booth.

It had become so quiet in the room that it seemed the entire class had stopped breathing. I felt a chill go down my spine. I worded the next question carefully.

Q. Who is the president of the country?
A. Abraham Lincoln *(subject shows signs of agitation).*
Q. Have you a middle name?
A. *(agitation increases markedly; frowns, seems confused; soft sound coming through his lips is barely audible)* "Ford."

I terminated the regression, bringing Wesley forward in time. He had been undergoing considerable stress and I felt that further questioning would be unwise at that time. The class clamored with eager questions. Someone asked if it might be possible for a subject to give a wrong name under stress? I admitted that *if* he were really Booth, he might well have become confused and given the name of the theatre in place of his own name. This was especially true, considering the event that had taken place at Ford's Theatre. Ford's Theatre in Washington, owned by John T. Ford, was closed after President Lincoln's assassination. Later turned into government offices, its roof collapsed, killing twenty people, in June, 1893, on the day of Edwin Booth's funeral. Since restored by the Department of the Interior as a National Historic Site, Ford's Theatre is open again to visitors.

Wesley was totally bewildered by the conversation until someone had the presence of mind to replay the tape. He listened to the soft voice intently; it was so unlike his own. It is a strange sensation to hear a voice on a tape recorder and, only because others have heard you utter the words, become convinced that you must have spoken them. "I couldn't have been Booth," Wesley protested, "I always thought that Lincoln was neat!"

I had no answer. I was afraid to hope that it might be true, because it made no sense. Although I had read of persons under hypnosis supposedly claiming to be some recognized personality, I had no firsthand knowledge. With Wesley's permission, I decided to investigate further.

Why should John Wilkes Booth, the infamous Shakespearian actor who had left his bloody mark upon the pages of history, return through the hypnotized lips of this young man? The question drove me in search of a logical answer.

At first, I experienced a sense of elation, believing that the regression might testify to Booth's return, but when I contemplated the task ahead, my enthusiasm dwindled to a mild depression. The deep depression was to come later.

2
DISCOURAGING DAYS

THERE WAS LITTLE PROGRESS FOR WEEKS ON END. AS Booth, Wesley was uninformative. His talking had increased, but he was evasive and at times seemed to resent my questions. He often retreated into a sullen silence if the questions were too personal.

Wesley himself was depressed. He wanted to help and was always willing to work with me, but he had no control over the Booth personality. I worried about the possible emotional damage to Wesley if we continued. To my knowledge, such an experiment had never been attempted when the previous life was an unbalanced personality. As nothing seemed to be happening to Wesley mentally, I continued to work with him, but Booth's memory was poor and did not improve. He seemed unable to remember the names of the theatres where he had performed.

During one of the regressions I asked Booth to name one of his brothers who had been a well-known actor.

23

"Larry," he answered.

Disgusted, I brought Wesley out of hypnosis and asked, "What was the name of John's brother?"

He replied, "Edwin . . . of course."

If Wesley was drawing from his memory storehouse, why didn't he give me the correct name? Obviously, he knew that it was Edwin, so what had caused him to say, "Larry?" On the other hand, if he really *was* Booth, why didn't he know the name of his brother?

The question was a puzzler, and a possibility crossed my mind. Suppose I had an imposter, someone who was merely claiming to be Booth? A friend of mine who had done some reading about the case, said that there were several persons who had made this claim.

Wesley seemed unconcerned and showed little interest in the tapes. He was convinced that it couldn't be true and that sooner or later I would have to reach the same conclusion. As my anxiety increased, I turned to prayer for guidance, and it seemed that something deep inside urged me on, in spite of conflicting logic.

There was some slight encouragement when Booth mentioned that he had been in Philadelphia on a special trip to see a man whom he referred to as "George." Although he was unable to remember the man's last name, he did say that while he was there he had gone to the theatre to see "Ed" perform.

Q. Who is Ed?
A. Don't you know?
Q. Could he be your brother?
A. *(curtly)* Of course! Certainly!

He elaborated on the incident only to say that he had slipped into the theatre during the performance, and that Edwin had been unaware of his presence.

I began to notice a strange cough plaguing Booth—

he often went into severe paroxysms. Wesley was having no difficulties with his throat or chest, and the results of a recent physical examination showed him to be in fine condition. When Booth's coughing became prolonged or unusually severe, I found that most of the time suggestion would stop it.

Other problems were increasing, however, and each regression became a war of nerves. Booth mumbled, and at times rambled incoherently. His evasive answers to my questions nearly drove me to distraction. How was it possible to make him talk if he was determined to refuse?

It is generally known that a person under hypnosis cannot be made to reveal anything he does not want to reveal, and if I had really reached Booth, he had much to hide. This situation had not arisen in other cases of prebirth regressions that I had directed or observed. I had to figure out a way to make him talk—but how?

If Wesley were making the whole thing up from the depths of his imagination, why was he talking about trivia? Why didn't he get right to the conspiracy? Certainly, if he were weaving a subconscious fantasy, he must long to play the hero's role in the big finale of Booth's life.

I began to realize that there had never been a regression like this one. In other cases of subjects regressed into former lives, it only had been necessary for them to talk. If they were lying or evading, who was to know? With Booth, I knew what I wanted discussed, and he was skirting the issue skillfully. Thus far, he had said nothing about President Lincoln.

My knowledge of Lincoln's assassination was vague. I knew that Booth had been an actor of some repute and that he had shot the President. I also knew that Booth was killed somewhere in the South. I remember that he had been considered mad, and that the shooting of Lincoln was the culmination of that madness. This was the extent of my knowledge. I was not, and never had been, a student of history.

Wesley, because of his youth, had a much closer view of the Lincoln tragedy. His school years were not in the past, as were mine. I questioned him at length and learned that he, too, had only a passing interest in the assassination and had done only the required reading about it. I began to be afraid that we were reaching a dead end. If Booth were to talk about what had already been written, what could it prove? On the other hand, if he were to reveal information that couldn't be verified, the problem remained the same.

From my first interest in prebirth recall, I have wondered if the subject knows who is questioning him, and in one of the regressions, I asked:

Q. Do you know who I am?
A. Don't you know who you are?
Q. Yes, I know, but I am wondering if you do.
A. *(a pause while he seems to be thinking)* You are Miss Carter, I believe, and you write stories, don't you?

This was not the first time that a hypnotized subject had given me an identity in a prebirth regression, but in my experience it is unusual. Because Booth had told me who he was, and I had been able to converse with him, I began to consider other methods to break down his reserve. Careful examination of the regression material led me to the conclusion that to Booth, I was merely a woman, and the role of a woman in the 1800s was very different from that of one in the 1970s. There was no equal footing in Booth's day, and a woman attempting to converse with a man about business matters would have been very much out of place. Of course he would not discuss the assassination with me. Perhaps that was the reason for my lack of success.

The thought crossed my mind that through suggestion I might be able to have Booth accept my voice as a man's voice. The idea was intriguing, yet if it worked there might be some danger to Wesley, and if he became confused, I could lose control. Another possible alternative came to mind. So far as I knew, it had not been used before, and if it were to fail, Wesley couldn't possibly be harmed. I decided it was worth a try.

My plan was to introduce a male voice to Booth with the help of one of my students. If I could manage to get him into an actual conversation with Booth, some breakthrough might result. Wesley was not told that anything unusual was to take place during the next regression.

3
THE BROOKS EXPERIMENT

THE MALE VOICE I PLANNED TO USE BELONGED TO BOB Brooks, an able student of mine in hypnosis. Bob was apprehensive, but agreed to accept my scheme. I, too, was nervous because success depended on whether I could introduce Bob and have Booth accept him naturally. I regressed Wesley to the point where, as Booth, he placed himself in Philadelphia in a theatre and was conversing with his stage manager.

Q. What are you talking about?
A. We are discussing some changes in the script. . . . (*abruptly*) But I must leave now as there is someone I have to meet . . . a meeting to attend.
Q. John, as you leave the theatre you will be meeting a friend; you will stop to talk to him. (*Bob speaks*)
Q. Hello, Wilkes—how've you been, Wilkes?
A. Are you addressing me, sir? . . . I assume I've met you before.

Q. Yes—not too long ago—we were drinking together. Shall we have a drink now?

A. Didn't I meet you before . . . in a tavern . . . was it Philadelphia?

Q. I believe that's right, Wilkes. We were talking about the terrible trouble the country is in now.

A. Perhaps I have you confused with . . . someone else. . . . What do you do, sir?

Q. I'm a commercial traveler.

A. I see . . . what is your ware?

Q. Harness—I travel around the country.

A. Should be profitable . . .

Q. Wouldn't deny that. Travel has advantages, but with this war going on it is difficult—depending where your sympathies lie.

A. Well . . . 'tis not a matter of sympathy in my case . . . but a matter of reputation.

Q. What are your personal feelings, outside of your reputation?

A. Don't know . . . don't give politics much thought . . . one should stand for one side . . . or other. . . . I find I can rarely, if ever, express my . . . personal viewpoint.

Q. Wouldn't one's viewpoint change if one saw the misery of the South?

A. It's a matter of . . . only stating that I don't . . . state my views. . . . One never can be certain . . . to whom one is talking.

Q. *(thinks a moment and decides to press the situation)* I have been talking to some of the men lately. . . .

A. *(grows noticeably still)* Oh?

Q. I've been talking to them about the Lincoln business.

A. *(Bob's words cause Booth to stiffen)* I believe that I shall have another drink *(brings imaginary glass to his lips and gulps audibly)*. Please excuse me while I give this some thought . . . *(puts his head into his hands; long silence follows)*.

30

While we waited for Booth to speak, Bob and I looked at each other. We had no idea what was going to happen. When the silence became prolonged, Bob offered Booth another drink.

A. No thank you . . . I want to be up to the performance this evening.

Q. What performance are you in this evening?

A. . . . Don't remember name of play . . . 'tis a lesser known work . . . relatively new. . . . You would enjoy it . . . hope you will attend. . . . Now, if you'll excuse me . . . I really must take my leave. . . . Good afternoon.

I considered the experiment interesting and thought that we had gained a measure of success, but the fact that Booth had terminated his own regression surprised me. I had never seen a hypnotized subject do this and was reminded of séances in which the entity speaks and, when finished, says "good-by." I had given some thought to the possibility that Booth might be a "disincarnate entity" rather than a "past-life recall," but if this were the case, wouldn't the entity *know* it was dead? Booth thought he was still living, and continued to guard his secrets.

Up to this time I had done very little reading about Booth, believing that if I did my own research, I would weaken my chances of getting an unbiased and acceptable story. I depended upon others to uncover facts, but found that they were not exact in their reporting. If I wanted to learn whether Booth *was* telling the truth, I would have to have more data. I compiled a list of books, but found that most were out-of-print "collectors' items." There were good references, however, and in one a passage caught my eye. The print almost leapt from the page as I read that Booth suffered from time to time from a bronchial condition, and periods of coughing and hoarseness had interrupted his career. This was further complicated by a voice problem, resulting from his poor preparation for stage work.

Here was evidence to support our case. If Wesley was drawing merely from stored information, *why should he develop the cough?* The reference to Booth's problem was so slight that it seemed unlikely it had ever been part of any class study. I made some notes of names, dates and places, so that I might recognize a clue, were he to offer one.

As I have mentioned, history was not a subject that interested me, nor was politics. Now it seemed I would have to learn something about both. I devised a plan to conceal the research I was doing by employing a scattered method of questioning. I could not allow Booth to construct a story from beginning to end; this would be too easy for him, and for me as well. I did not want to risk introducing, by suggestion, any facts that I had gathered.

Asking questions in widely separated areas represented work, but seemed to offer the greatest protection for my research. Once I had enough information, I could go back over the tapes and piece the story together in jigsaw puzzle fashion. I couldn't possibly have foreseen the endless hours this work would require.

4
THE REAL VOICE OF MR. BOOTH

A DRAMATIC TURNING POINT IN THE CASE CAME ON SEP-tember 3, 1969. Bob Brooks was standing by just in case I might want to work him into the conversation, but as it turned out, I didn't need him.

Among the witnesses that night was a skeptical news-man who was so blinded by his prejudice against reincar-nation that he refused to believe what he saw. I realized later that he had come to see a hoax and his mind was closed.

The regression began:

Q. It is 1864 and you are entering Ford's Theatre; tell me what you see.
A. I have walked in . . . the stage is ahead of me. . . . All of the draperies have been removed.
Q. Why has this been done?
A. There is no show right now and no scenery.
Q. What are you doing here?

A. *(voice suddenly heavier)* I am going to be performing here soon . . . within a few weeks. . . . I arrived in Washington early . . . I have preparations due . . . business to take care of.

Q. What kind of business?

A. Oh, highly private.

Q. Why are you in Ford's Theatre?

A. I just want to look around . . . look it over.

Q. Haven't you seen it before?

A. Oh yes, but I haven't played here in a while. *(voice deepens; speaks with a stage accent)* It's good to get the feel of the building . . . every theatre has a certain feel . . . an air about it. Some say that particular ghosts prevail there . . . if one believes in ghosts.

Q. Do you believe in ghosts, John?

A. Well, I must admit that there are several things that have happened to me . . . that are rather strange . . . but I can't attribute them to ghosts or spirits.

Q. Let us get back to the reason for your being in Ford's Theatre.

A. There will be certain special performances given here.

Q. Special?

A. Of course . . . being in Washington we must entertain the dignitaries . . . or shall I say the Congress? And then, of course, there is the President.

Q. The President? What does he have to do with it?

A. Well . . . you know the President comes to the theatre. *(haughtily, his tone of voice clipped and cynical)* I shall try to make him . . . more welcome this time.

The regression was quite lengthy and I have included only the dialogue that had to do with the voice change. When Booth spoke out he was heard clearly by everyone in the room. We were never to hear that first small, almost inaudible, voice again. After I had completed the theatrical part of the regression, I suggested to Booth that he was alone and writing an entry into his diary. He rapidly wrote the following lines:

> *Today, talked to Masters about his role in the plan. He agreed to follow through with his part of the bargain and felt that the best thing would be to follow through with the other plans made at the last meeting.*

The writing meant nothing to me. I was unable to find any mention of anyone named "Masters." I slipped the paper into an envelope and filed it away; it was to be several months before I could place this vital bit of information into its proper context.

I should explain here how it is possible to get a subject to write while under hypnosis. A word of caution—it is a risky experiment—but in this case I thought it had to be tried. After suggesting to Booth that he is alone, I tell him that in a moment I will ask him to open his eyes. I place a tablet on his lap and a pen in his hand, and tell him that when he opens his eyes he will see only the paper and the words he is writing. Then I suggest that he open his eyes and begin the writing, and that when finished, he lay the pen down.

When working with a subject in a prebirth regression, it is necessary to limit his seeing to the items I have mentioned. Otherwise, as in the case of Booth, were he to see his surroundings with eyes accustomed only to the 1800s, he might enter into hysteria or shock and the hypnotist would lose control. In the first experiments with Booth, I neglected to tell him that he would be able to see the writing. I had mentioned only the paper, and the result was a scrawl that was difficult to decipher. It took a while to discover my error. I realized the problem while playing the tapes back, and once this was corrected, the writing improved.

Booth wrote the following during the next regression:

I find today that there has been more discussion about Stewart. I find this to be unconvincing. I see no reason to consider him. I do feel that others have more to offer in the way of help.

Again, I checked through my notes and material and found no mention of anyone named "Stewart." I wondered if he could have meant "Seward" but I had no way of knowing and did not want to offer him a name that he had not yet given. The second paper was filed with the first.

Many people were urging me to confront Booth with the assassination and demand that he talk about it, but I was reluctant to do this; I was on uncertain ground until Booth was ready to talk. I believed that I needed to know more before attempting to take him through the trauma of the assassination.

There was no doubt that Booth did not think he was dead. He conversed easily and his ready wit and charm were felt by every woman in the room. There was often such a large attendance at the regressions that some spectators had to sit on the floor, but however great the interest, we seemed to be getting nowhere until a regression took an unusual turn and set the stage for subsequent exchanges.

I had been talking to Booth about his work in the theatre and he had told me he had to go there that evening. We were making light conversation when he suddenly said: "I don't think I will go to the theatre this evening."

Q. Why aren't you going? Are you with someone?
A. With you . . . or at least I would like to be.
Q. Do you know who I am?

A. Why, I believe that your name is Mary . . . isn't it?
Q. *(warmly)* Yes, it is.

We entered into a very comical situation. Booth began to insist I join him on the floor in front of the fireplace. I had no idea where he thought we were, and in trying to keep the conversation alive, said, "This is a very nice place you have."

Booth turned to me with a quizzical look, "Surely you know it isn't mine . . . it sounds very strange to hear you say that. . . . You have a room here also . . . have you not?"

"Yes, but I like your room better!"

"My *room!*" he exploded, and after a long silence demanded, "Are you making fun of me?"

I had to be quick to correct my slip of the tongue and make him think I had been teasing him. While doing so, I realized we must be in the parlor of a boarding house. Booth's veneer of charm returned as he asked, "Would you like a glass of sherry?"

"Yes, thank you."

He went through the motions of pouring the sherry and, handing me an imaginary glass, said, "Sherry is nice after a meal, don't you agree?"

"Yes, it is, John."

"It is so peaceful here . . . in front of the fire *(voice very drowsy, drifting as if thinking aloud)* "Makes one . . . almost forget . . . the troubles that are besetting us now."

"Yes, we have many problems." I hoped to lead him into a discussion of the country's difficulties.

"Well . . . I wouldn't say that we have many problems . . . but we have one very large problem. . . .One has to eliminate the cause in order to solve the problem . . . wouldn't you agree?"

Although I was quick to agree with him, Booth

abruptly changed the subject. It was as if he realized he had been talking too much.

Comparing the Booth regression with others I have undertaken, no subject has ever been more expressive with his voice and hands. His hands fascinated me, and he used them beautifully to emphasize his conversation. Wesley also uses his hands when he talks, but he lacks the grace of Booth.

I had read that Booth moved in social circles. In later regressions he began to name names, but they were difficult to trace. Booth had attended many lavish affairs in and around Washington, Philadelphia and Baltimore. His manners were not those of an aimless playboy, and he was accepted at a time when actors generally were regarded as "crude and vulgar." His charm and good looks were his passport.

When I discussed this with Booth, he replied sarcastically, "For the most part the description is a fair one!"

Booth loved the ladies. He escorted the well-to-do, as well as women who were regarded as nobodies. Having drawn me into the conversation, and accepting me as the young lady of his choice, Booth finally handed me the key that was to take me back into his life during the 1800s. I suggested that he and I were attending a party; I supplied the year and allowed him to select the particular occasion. He moved easily into his part, treating me as if I were the young lady he was escorting. I tried this several times and noted with interest that his behavior changed according to the personality of his companion. When he had selected a party, my usual question was, "Do you see anyone you know here tonight?"

Booth, with closed eyes, would move his head from side to side and look around a room filled with people that only he could see. His eyeballs moved beneath the lids, and at times he would converse briefly with someone who evidently had addressed him. His part of the dialogue would go something like this:

"Oh, the usual . . . working very hard and, of course . . . traveling a great deal."

Sometimes he would introduce me, but if he assumed that I knew a person, he would not. I had no way of knowing who he thought I was until he either introduced me or called me by name, usually by a first name only. Very few women of Booth's acquaintance are known to history. One exception was the lovely Bessie Hale, daughter of Senator John Parker Hale from New Hampshire. Secretly, I hoped to find myself in a situation where he would identify me as Bessie, because she had been very close to Booth.

Each regression was a puzzling network of clues, and it was necessary to review a tape about six times before I was satisfied I had not missed anything important. This was a tedious process, for something that seemed trivial at the time of taping later assumed significance as more information was released.

With the passing of time I became very close to John Wilkes Booth. I was sensitive to his moods and could detect evasiveness in his voice. I learned that Booth seldom lied, but was a master in the art of evading the truth. The "actor" was the most difficult for me to cope with, as at times he drew a curtain about himself. This has been commented upon by persons who knew him.

For a long time I had no reason to believe that Booth had died anywhere but at the Garrett farm, and while working on that premise, realized that finding facts not known to history was going to be the task that I must undertake. The question was, "How?"

5
OUT-OF-LIFE HYPNOSIS

AS MY READING AND KNOWLEDGE OF HISTORY EXPANDED, I learned that, in spite of what appeared to be positive identification of dental work and an old surgical scar, there still existed some doubt whether Booth was the man who died at the Garrett farm. When I read of the possibility of an escape, I became elated, but I hardly dared allow myself to think about it. If it *were* true; if I *had* succeeded in bringing Booth back, he would be able to supply the details.

I decided to place Wesley under hypnosis, using a different technique of taking him (by suggestion) *back* to, but not *into* the Booth life. This is common practice in prebirth regression, but Wesley responded strangely, moving his body about in the chair and saying in an agitated voice, "I don't see anything . . . I don't know where I am." No previous subject had behaved in this manner; he seemed to be struggling, and I quickly brought him out of the hypnotic state.

When I next tried this technique, I simply asked the question, "How old were you when you left your physical life as John Wilkes Booth?"

I could feel my mouth become dry, and spectators began to shift restlessly. After what seemed like an agonizing wait, two words came slowly, very softly, from Wesley's lips:

"Thirty-nine."

I became overly anxious then, and placed Wesley into the Booth life, suggesting that it was 1867.

"Where are you now, John?" I asked. We waited again, but there was no reply and I had to terminate the regression.

Someone who possessed a great deal of common sense pointed out my blunder. Certainly if Booth had lived beyond the assassination, he would have had to change his name, and I had called him "John." I was chagrined.

The following week passed slowly while many thoughts raced through my mind. If Booth had, in fact, escaped death at the Garrett farm, how had he managed his escape? If he had given his age as "thirty-six," I would have suspected a slip of the tongue; he was twenty-six, nearly twenty-seven, when he supposedly met his end—but *"thirty-nine?"*

As I read once more the account of his death at the Garrett farm, it seemed so final. I began to doubt my own sanity and to wonder how I had entertained the thought that somehow he might have escaped and lived.

On the night of the next regression, I was admittedly nervous. Everything depended on the outcome, and I had reached the point of "scrap it, or save it." If Booth had deliberately lied to me, there was little to be gained by continuing the experiment.

I should explain that there can be real danger to a subject when he has been taken to the out-of-life state of hypnosis. A British author, Henry Blythe, writes of his experience in *The Three Lives of Naomi Henry.* The book was written in the era of "Bridey Murphy," and Mr. Blythe describes the removal of a subject from her supposed lifetime. He was in the process of having her relive her death scene when her pulse slowly faded. Having taken the precaution of holding his finger on her pulse, he managed within seconds to suggest that she was living and well. Suppose he had been careless—who knows what the outcome might have been?

Bob Brooks is studying to become a doctor, and I asked him to place a stethoscope upon Wesley's chest during the out-of-life episodes. With this precaution, I was ready to begin the regression.

I started off with a party scene to get Booth into a talkative mood before I removed him from his lifetime. Only a scrap of information came at that time, but what a priceless scrap!

Q. Where were you when you left your physical body?
A. Not in this country . . . not in America.
Q. *Where* were you?
A. Cal . . . Calay . . . Cal . . . ay . . .

Calais, France? Was it possible? If Booth had died in France, then he would have known how to speak French! Wesley later assured me that he had no knowledge of the language.

Another week passed uneventfully. Meanwhile, I had talked with Hazelle Hunt, a first cousin of mine who knew some French. I had an idea, and together we devised a plan.

During the next regression (again in a party situation), I introduced Booth to Hazelle. I described her as young and pretty, telling him that she had recently returned from a trip to France. I called her "Suzanne" and waited for his response. Booth's face remained impassive and I couldn't tell what he was thinking. I added, "She

43

has heard of you, and would very much like an auto-graph."

A. *(stiffens and is noticeably irritated)* It does seem that I can never escape them!

Q. *(brightly)* Here she is now. Suzanne, this is Mr. Booth.

S. Bon soir, Monsieur Booth.

A. *(smiles)* Good evening.

S. *(speaks several words in French about her happiness at having met him)*

A. I am sorry . . . but you will have to speak English.

This regression was disappointing in one respect only—Booth refused to speak French. But he had asked Suzanne what part of France she visited, and she replied that she had visited Paris and Calais. At the mention of Calais, Booth's interest appears to quicken.

A. *(whispers nervously to himself)* "I see . . . Calais. . . hmmmm."

Wesley, as Booth, gave Suzanne an autograph—"To Suzanne from J. W. Booth."

6
A VERY STRANGE STORY

As Booth's strange story continued to unfold, I could not deny the possibility of his reincarnation. In the out-of-life state, he often supplied information that only served to whet my appetite.

Q. You are now beyond your life as John Wilkes Booth, and you may talk to me freely. No one has the power to hurt you. What name did you use when you left the country after the assassination?
A. Sullivan . . . William Sullivan
Q. How old were you when you left your physical body?

[I often repeated a question to avoid misunderstanding; sometimes Booth contradicted himself, but in this case he replied as before, "Thirty-nine."]

Q. How long did you remain in the country before leaving it?

A. Several months.

Q. Where did you stay?

A. San Francisco.

Q. From where did you sail when you left the country?

A. *(no answer)*

Q. From what *city* did you sail?

A. San Francisco.

Q. What was the name of the ship?

A. St. Margaret . . .

Q. Do you recall the name of the captain?

A. *(mumbles)* . . . not English . . . not certain . . .

Q. When you left, was it still 1865?

A. Yes . . . late November . . . early December.

Q. Where did you eventually land?

A. Portsmouth, England.

Q. When you went aboard ship at San Francisco, were you using the name William Sullivan?

A. No . . . I was James Benton.

Q. Did you use any disguise?

A. No one would have recognized me . . . I had changed.

Q. What do you mean?

A. I had changed certain things . . . I had shaved my beard, and I used make-up on my hair . . . I walked with a limp.

Q. Were you living in Calais at the time of your death?

A. Yes.

Q. Can you give me the name of the cemetery where your body is buried?

A. *Le Jardin de Plaisir.*

Q. What does that mean in English?

A. The Garden of Pleasure.

Q. Did any of your family know that you lived after the assassination?

A. Mother and Ed knew.

Q. Who else in your family knew?

A. No one.

Q. How did your mother and Edwin come to know that you were living?

A. By accident . . . in London.

Q. How did it happen?

A. Well . . . Ed saw me, and after he had seen me . . . we visited for a short while.

Q. Where were your mother and Edwin when they saw you?

A. In a carriage.

Q. Wasn't it a terrible shock to your mother?

A. She was very happy . . . Ed was upset.

Q. He was upset?

A. Very upset!

Q. Why?

A. He wanted me dead *(Booth's voice breaks with emotion).*

Q. Now, let's go back. Were you at any time in the barn at the Garrett farm?

A. No!

Q. Were you with Davy Herold?

A. He was to come shortly after . . . but I had to leave . . . he hadn't yet arrived.

Q. Were you injured in any way?

A. My leg was injured.

Q. How did it happen?

A. I was shot . . . I had a bullet wound.

Q. Who shot you?

A. I don't know.

Q. Where did it happen?

A. At the theatre . . . on my way out.

A. Did you fall from the stage?

A. Not from the stage . . . no.

Q. Where did you fall?

A. I fell onto the stage.

Q. When you were hit by the bullet?

A. No, when I jumped.

Q. Did you trip over something?

A. I don't know whether I tripped or not . . . I just know that I fell.

Q. Who removed the bullet from your leg?

A. The . . . Doctor Carter.

Q. How were you able to reach Doctor Carter?

A. Carriage.

Q. Was there anyone with you?

A. Mr. Richards.

Q. Who was he?

A. I had never met him before.

I have given a synopsis of several regressions; the information was agonizingly slow in coming. When I reviewed the material, I found much to ponder, but the story was illogical and it didn't improve with further study. If Wesley were weaving a fantasy, why was it so farfetched? Why had he veered from the known facts of the case? I searched the available literature to determine whether to believe any part of it.

I could find no history that said Booth had been shot; he was reportedly injured when he leapt from the box onto the stage. There also was no mention of a "Mr. Richards"—the only "Richards" I found was Major A. C. Richards, Superintendent of the Metropolitan Police— an unlikely accomplice! And Booth said that he had not met Mr. Richards before the assassination, which made no sense at all. What kind of fool would "just happen" to drive by in a carriage and stop to pick up a wounded man running out of a theatre?

One interesting source of information, some of it useful, was Izola Forrester's book, *This One Mad Act*. In it, Mrs. Forrester claims to have been the granddaughter of John Wilkes Booth. She does not believe that Booth was killed at the Garrett farm and seems to think he escaped from the barn. It doesn't seem possible that someone would have been willing to take Booth's place, knowing *he* could not escape, but at the time I read Mrs. Forrester's book I was grasping at straws, and hoped she was right.

Many historians have discounted Izola Forrester's relationship to Booth, and in most of the accounts there is no mention of Booth's ever having married. Mrs. Forrester's claim that he had married her grandmother, and that the Booth family knew of it, loses credibility in the light of a letter to John from his mother, Mary Ann Booth, hinting at her son's relationship with Bessie Hale.

"Not exactly a secret," Mrs. Booth writes, "as Edwin was told by someone you were paying great attention to a young lady in Washington. . . . Her father, I see, has his appointment; would he give his consent? You can but ask . . . you know in my partial eyes you are a fit match for any woman . . . "

Would she write such a letter if she knew that John was already married, much less that he had a child? There were many questions that so far seemed unanswerable. Izola Forrester's book was published in 1937, many years after the death of Booth's immediate family, leaving no one to challenge her statements.

In one of the regressions I asked a direct personal question: "Are you married, Mr. Booth?"

He thought for a moment and replied, "You can say that Mr. Booth is not married."

There was enough emphasis on "Mr. Booth" to cause me to wonder if he might not have been married under another name. I had asked the question in the guise of a writer for a magazine. Booth responded and, in the out-of-life state, named his wife "Izola."

He said the name slowly, breaking it into three syllables, "I . . . zo . . . la," and spoke so softly that I had to record it onto another machine and increase the volume to be sure of what he had said. The name Izola is not a common one, and it is unlikely that it could be found by anyone reading the usual accounts of the assassination.

When I asked Booth where his marriage had taken place, he told me, "Clinton, Maryland." This was surprising, because Mrs. Forrester placed the marriage in Cos Cob, Connecticut, January 9, 1859. In her book she writes that it was not compulsory in those days to record either marriages or births at the town hall. The only vital statistics kept were deaths. Mrs. Forrester claims that her grandmother and Booth were married by a Reverend Peleg Weaver, but had no document to prove it. "This marriage was not in Cos Cob, Connecticut as my grandmother Izola Forrester supposed," wrote Gail Merrifield, great-great grandaughter of John Wilkes Booth. "Cos Cob was merely where Rev. Peleg Weaver, the minister who she stated performed the ceremony, spent his last days, and where his descendants remained. Rev. Weaver was somewhere else in 1859. . . ." (Gail Merrifield became the custodian of the John Wilkes Booth archives; held a birth certificate for Ogarita Booth born in 1859.) Booth could not remember the name he had used in his marriage to Izola, but thought that it might have been "Brayton." He was certain of the first name, "James." As Booth had used a number of names, it is not surprising that he had some difficulty remembering them.

While reading Stanley Kimmel's book, *The Mad Booths of Maryland,* I came across other data to discount Mrs. Forrester's claim of a Connecticut marriage. Kimmel writes that Booth was working in Richmond, Virginia at that time, and a check of his working schedule would demonstrate that he could not have been away for the length of time required to make a trip to Cos Cob without someone knowing of his absence. Kimmel cites family letters that indicate the family had no knowledge of such a union, stressing especially the letter from John's mother. My research into the marriage might have ended here had Kimmel not written: "It was noted that Booth did go to Baltimore about three months later to attend his sister's wedding." This would have been the marriage of Asia Booth to John Sleeper Clarke.

An idea occurred to me. I consulted a map and confirmed that Clinton, Maryland is a short distance from Baltimore, and would have been on the route from Richmond to Baltimore; Booth was acting in Richmond at the time.

Now I was convinced that Izola's daughter by Booth had been born out of wedlock and I questioned him about the marriage.

Q. John, I want you to tell me about your marriage to Izola.

A. I met Izola . . . I believe that it was in Baltimore . . . one evening immediately after a performance. . . . I found her to be quite attractive . . . we became well acquainted . . . but I felt that it would be unwise to marry her.

We continued to see each other . . . sometimes under a certain amount of cover. . . . After several months, she insisted on some sort of permanent arrangement. She felt that anything else would have been . . . as she put it . . . sinful. I told her that I was unable to marry . . . that I had many obligations . . . and would not be able to settle down to take care of a home. She threatened a scandal . . . because she was going to have a child.

I consented to a marriage . . . with one exception—I would not use my proper name . . . as I thought that would have been unwise. . . . She would have no way of causing me difficulty . . . and there would be no proof that I had been married. . . . Since she came to realize that there would be no other way in which she could marry me . . . she consented.

We were married one or two months later when I

was free to make the trip to Maryland. My wife realized later that I had tricked her to an extent . . . but
there was nothing she could do about it. She was a
very nice woman and I still had a certain affection for
her . . . but I believed that she was better off with
the . . . arrangement that we had.

Q. Did you ever see the child?

A. On occasion . . . shortly after her birth.

A letter to a friend from a Mrs. Elijah Rogers of Harford
County, Md. establishes the fact that Izola bore a daughter fathered by Booth and states that there was also a son
whose name was Alonso.

Parts of the Forrester book were noteworthy in the
light of Booth's remarks. It was tradition in the family
that Edwin and his mother had been riding in a carriage
in London after the assassination and had seen a man
start to cross the street; Edwin recognized him as his
brother, John.

According to Blanche Dis de Bar Booth, niece of
John Wilkes, in a report to the International News Service, there were stories in the family of her uncle's surviv-
al after the assassination; they include one in which John
met his mother in San Francisco about a year after the
assassination and related the details of his escape to her.
His mother continued to tell members of the family that
she had visited her son and that he had given her certain
information.

Mrs. Forrester described a house standing on San
Francisco's Telegraph Hill. The house was badly dilapi-
dated and shunned by older residents of the area because
they considered it to be haunted by the spirit of John
Wilkes Booth. Mrs. Forrester goes on to say that newspapers carried a story reviving rumors that Booth had been
secretly in the city, and for a time had occupied the old
dwelling; a search of papers dated a year after the war un-

covered accounts of a "mysterious stranger" who roamed about only after dark and was described as being aloof, handsome and cloaked. Although Booth was not named, the description fitted him remarkably well.

It is interesting that, according to a California newspaper, Booth's brother, Joseph, who was a Wells Fargo messenger covering the area around Telegraph Hill, disappeared from San Francisco shortly before the assassination. When he arrived in New York after the assassination he was arrested, interrogated about John Wilkes' affairs of which he knew nothing, and finally released. Less fortunate were John Sleeper Clarke, Asia's husband, and Junius Booth (another brother), who were charged with complicity and served jail sentences in the Old Capitol Prison where the accused conspirators had been confined.

The Booth family was tormented after the death of President Lincoln—even Edwin who, though not imprisoned, was under continuous surveillance. From prison, Junius wrote to Edwin with optimism that "we must use philosophy—'tis a mere matter of time. . . . I feel sure time will bring all things right—that is, as right as we have any right to expect."

Asia Booth Clarke stated her family's position differently. In her book entitled *The Unlocked Book: A Memoir of John Wilkes Booth*, she wrote, "Those who have passed through such an ordeal, if there are any such, may be quick to forgive, slow to resent; they never relearn to trust in human nature, they never resume their old place in the world, and they forget only in death."

7
BOOTH SPEAKS OF THE THEATRE

JOHN WILKES BOOTH EARNED A GOOD LIVING AS AN actor—$20,000 a year was a lot of money in those days—but what did he really think of his theatrical career?

When I removed Wesley from his own lifetime and led him slowly across a time bridge into the personality of Booth, it was as though unseen fingers explored his face and began to reshape his features into those of an older man. The network of minute facial muscles tightened, the jaw drooped slightly, the facial expression underwent a dramatic change and his face became longer, the mouth assuming a serious mien.

Wesley had been sprawled in the chair; now he twisted slightly to raise his body to an upright position. He straightened his shoulders and inclined his head slightly forward. When he answered my questions his voice was rich and full, his accent slightly British. I had presented myself as an interviewer from a magazine.

Q. Mr. Booth, how many years have you been performing in Shakespearean roles?

A. I'm not at all sure, but it's been a long time ⋮ . . . many years . . . since I was sixteen or seventeen.

Q. Are you happy being an actor?

A. Oh . . . happy enough, I guess.

Q. Do you mind if I ask you a personal question, Mr. Booth?

A. And if I do not wish to answer? (*smiling*) then . . . I will not answer.

Q. It has been said that you are a "ladies' man." Do you believe this to be true?

A. I find women fascinating. . . . while it is true that women are less knowledgeable than men, this only makes them more interesting to me.

Q. Do you find Shakespearean roles difficult?

A. Oh yes . . . Shakespeare is always difficult.

Q. I should have thought that, with your experience, it might have become routine.

A. Never . . . although I'm not sure I can explain. . . . I do not quite understand it myself . . . but every time I play in Shakespeare . . . it is as if for the first time. It is something different every time . . . that is why I enjoy Shakespeare.

Q. Have you a show this evening?

A. No . . . not tonight. . . . I never do a show on Sunday.

Q. What theatre are you presently performing in?

A. I believe the name is . . . Park . . . or Royal . . . James . . . ? I don't know, I play in so many. . . . It's not really very important.

Q. I think it strange that you don't know the name of the theatre.

A. (*sharply*) The name of the theatre does not interest me. . . . I have no need to know the name. . . . If I had to know . . . then I would know!

Booth's faulty memory continued to plague the regressions. One might assume that an actor would have an exceptional ability to memorize and recall, but as I read more about Booth I learned that he had been prone to making errors on stage, and had been hissed off more than once for his failure to remember lines. He was known to have mispronounced words and been slovenly in speech. He was impatient and it seems that he did not take the time necessary to prepare himself for his theatrical career. As the regressions continued, Booth's inability to remember names of theatres where he had performed puzzled me.

Q. Wouldn't there be a possibility of getting into the wrong theatre if you didn't know the name?

A. Well . . . I rarely play a town that has more than one theatre. There is usually one meeting hall . . . one theatre, or what-have-you, and it would be difficult to confuse it with anything else. . . . If one is in doubt, one always can walk up to someone and ask, "What theatre is Mr. Booth playing tonight?" . . . (*sarcastically*) Everyone is more than happy to oblige.

Booth often flashed out with repressed anger and a dislike for theatre audiences. He confirmed that he hated acting and only did it as a means to make money. A conversation during a party scene sharply defined this statement. Booth was candid and sarcastic, and many glasses of punch caused him to talk freely. A slight slurring of his words was apparent during the regression.

Q. Do you value your acting career, John?

A. For one reason only . . . monetary gain.

Q. That's an honest answer.

A. I don't know whether or not it is honest . . . I guess

57

I could have said, "My reason for being in the theatre is that I can't stand not to be on stage, performing!". . . . or, perhaps, "I am an actor because the sound of the applause is so invigorating!" (*in stage voice, with great exaggeration*) I l-o-v-e the audience!

Q. I can understand how you feel.

A. However, (*bitterly*) . . . I don't really like the audience . . . they are no more than cattle . . . no more than swine . . . feeding on another's gift. They become excited . . . so thrilled, so transported!

Q. Do you hate people that much, John?

A. (*more soberly*) Not all people . . . only the majority. You see, when I meet someone . . . I have a choice . . . I can continue to see and talk to that someone . . . or I may leave. In the theatre, I have no choice . . . I can't choose who's there . . . that is . . . a person may come to see me as many times as he wishes . . . I have no control.

Q. But, if it were not for the public, you wouldn't be able to earn a living.

A. (*sharply*) I don't have to *like* them!

For a while I could not understand why Booth, a successful actor, should have such a dislike for the theatre. Perhaps it was a sense of inadequacy in his performances, or his throat trouble, which recurred from time to time causing him great distress.

How does Wesley feel about all this? I am asked the question often, and have to answer that he is calm—almost indifferent. He rarely listens to the tapes and seems to function normally in his work and everyday life. His revelations as Booth do not appear to have affected him. Many have said they would lack the courage to undergo long hours of hypnosis. Wesley believes, as do I, that we must complete this study to the best of our abilities. If there are repercussions, they will have to be absorbed as they come.

In the out-of-life segments of Wesley's hypnotic regressions, animation ceased. He became still, slumping into the chair, and although the Booth expressions persisted, his voice slowed and sank to a monotone, losing most of its rich tonal quality.

I should mention that Wesley's normal rhythm of speech varies noticeably from Booth's, that is to say, the spaces between words are much longer in Booth's speaking than in Wesley's. Booth seems to weigh his words more carefully. It was some time before I realized that the slow tempo and the long take were in vogue for actors of Booth's day, rather than the increased tempo and more natural responses of our time.

John Wilkes Booth was a man of many faces, but his stage roles were secondary to his performances on the real stage of life. It has been recorded that he had interests outside the theatre, for the most part unsuccessful business ventures. His activities were difficult to trace because of the extensive travel necessary to an actor's career. Booth used this as an entrée to the South for undercover business and conspiracy. He took part in blockade running, and for six months before the assassination was plotting to kidnap President Lincoln.

Some historians have described Booth as mad and stupid, but I cannot agree. As the tapes accumulated and I gradually pieced together the parts of his many-sided personality, he emerged as a man of genius and intelligence. If he was a pawn in the hands of others, he came to know this only too well.

8
JOHN, ASIA AND EDWIN

LOVED ONES GRIEVE FOR THE VICTIM OF AN assassination, but the family of the assassin must bear sorrow alone, sharing only guilt and the terrible question. . . . "Why?" Memories of happier days are locked in aching hearts; stories cannot be told. Asia Booth Clarke's *The Unlocked Book* was published many years after the tragedy of her brother, John Wilkes Booth, had blackened the family's name and broken their hearts.

That the sister's fears for her brother were realized some time before the assassination is apparent from her description of a conversation during which he told her that he was smuggling quinine to the South.

"I knew now," writes Asia, "that my hero was a spy, a blockade runner, a rebel! I set the terrible words before my eyes, and knew that each one meant death. . . . I found myself trying to think with less detestation of those two despicable characters in history, Major André and Benedict Arnold."

Perhaps no one in the Booth family was as close to John as was Asia. Disagreements during later years when she knew the extent of her brother's activities did not diminish her love for him, and as she lay dying she entrusted to a friend the material that was to become her book. In it is exposed a side of Booth not touched upon by most historians who have written about his life and crime.

Asia writes that John was called "Billy Bow Legs," when he was very young. He had been called "Billy" for some time afterward, and it interested me that Booth, when I questioned him, remembered being "Billy," but not "Bow Legs." He was known to have been self-conscious about his legs and usually wore a long coat or cloak to cover this one defect of his otherwise athletic frame.

Q. Were you ever called "Billy Bow Legs?"
A. (*indignantly*) Who would have called me such a name?
Q. This was a long time ago; weren't you called "Billy?"
A. I can remember being called "Billy" when I was a very small child. I always preferred to be called "John," but they couldn't seem to understand that . . . I just can't remember being called such an ugly nickname (*note of resignation comes into his voice*), but perhaps I was.
Q. Your sister writes of such an incident [a slip of the tongue on my part].
A. Writes . . . ? (*confused*)
Q. Don't worry about it. Did Asia used to write often?
A. We wrote poems and rhymes, many, many . . . so many years ago, when I was a very small child.
Q. Were you and Asia close, John?
A. I loved her very much. As I grew older I was not able to get home often . . . we seemed to grow apart, even more as Edwin grew older and liked me less and less. . . . He tried to convince Asia that I was no

good . . . perhaps he succeeded . . . because we didn't have the joy and fun of our early years, not when Edwin was there. . . . Perhaps that's why I didn't go home more often.

Q. Don't you think it might have been because your ideas changed, and she was afraid for you?

A. That's possible. . . . Sometimes when I talked to her privately, she agreed with me . . . it seemed that she liked me more than Edwin, and yet she followed Edwin . . . I never understood that.

Q. Did you discuss your activities in the South with her?

A. No . . . nothing specific, just the war in general— life in general.

Q. Shortly before the assassination, did you give her something to keep?

A. I gave her several things.

Q. Among the things that you gave her, were there letters?

A. I was thinking more of presents, but . . . yes, many times when I came home I'd bring correspondence: a full diary which I had no place to keep. It became far too big and bulky to carry everywhere . . . I couldn't take much with me . . . there wasn't room. Asia kept many things where I thought they would be safe . . . where no one would notice . . . but I found out later that they had been disturbed.

Q. You know that she suffered a great deal because of what you had done, don't you, John?

A. It never seemed that she would be in any danger. Why should they bother her when I was the one to blame? . . . Years later I heard about it and was shocked.

Sorrow shaded Booth's words. His face was drawn as he talked; his voice had dropped almost to a whisper as emotions tugged at him. I thought of how differently we would lead our lives if only we could understand that death does not end our yesterdays. Life is a continuing thread upon which we string the beads of our earthly incarnations, each lifetime molding the next.

Many times, as I sat talking to John, I was reminded of the words of a great Indian teacher who said, "Each soul is struggling to be good, but 'good' is only as he sees it." Surely, in the Booth case, I caught a glimpse of the truth behind these words, the essence of what is good, even in the heart of an assassin.

In the next regression Booth gave a vivid description of his older brother, Edwin, who but for one dark page in history might have been the better known of the two. There is evidence of great rivalry between the brothers. It is interesting to see Edwin Booth through John's eyes and share his one-sided, slanted insight into the character of the famous actor. John was spoiled, and resented discipline from Edwin.

Q. John, I want you to tell me about your brother, Edwin.

A. When I started in the theatre, it was under the guidance of Edwin. He took it upon himself to teach me all there was to know about acting. I suppose I should have looked up to him and followed his direction . . . he was older than I . . . but I found that not everything he said was true. He had his style . . . and it seemed as if he was trying to mold me to be just like him. This was not my way . . . it was not my way to be just like anyone, so I assume that I rebelled to some extent. . . . Some of his ways of acting were all right, but I found some other of his ways inadequate for me. . . . We both drank, but many times Edwin drank so much that he was incapable of going on stage and performing. I found this disgusting. . . . Drinking is one thing . . . but to let it burden your life so that you cannot perform the tasks set out for you! We disagreed on that point, and we disagreed about acting.

Later I gained some notice in the theatre . . . so did Edwin, but at times it seemed that I was more in demand than he. He became jealous and this only led to more drinking.

Another thing . . . when father died, although I am quite certain that Ed felt some sorrow, he acted . . . I don't know, almost as if he were glad to see him go. . . . And he didn't keep in touch with mother . . . would go for long periods of time without letting her know that he was alive. . . . Mother didn't care for me too much, but I tried to do some things for her when I could. I, at least, wrote occasionally . . . I don't think Edwin ever did.

When I learned that Booth had died in Calais, I asked him if there might have been any jewelry—a ring perhaps—buried with him. He answered that there had been a gold charm and a chain which he had carried for years. It had been given him by his father. I questioned Booth about this ornament.

Q. Tell me about the charm and chain that you carried.
A. Oh, that belonged to father . . . it was given to him many years ago, and was to have been mine when he died. . . . Edwin was in charge of his things, and kept it . . . why, I don't know, he had no use for it, he didn't like it much. . . . He kept it because he had to, I guess . . . that was Ed.
Q. How did you manage to get it?
A. I asked Edwin for it upon several occasions, and sometimes he would say he didn't have it . . . when it was obvious that he did have it, or if it was in sight, he would say that he wanted to wait until I had reached a certain age, or when something specific happened. When I pressed the point he would say

"Well . . . I don't know . . ." At last I saw an opportunity and I took it . . . it had been promised to me and by all rights it was mine. Ed never said anything about it . . . it was more of a game to him . . . he always liked to play games and some of them didn't make much sense . . . some were harmful . . . sometimes his games hurt others, but he didn't seem to care as long as he was able to play his game! I suppose to him, life was nothing but a play. . . . There was no reality for him.

As I listened to John describing Edwin, I wondered how some of the other famous men in history would measure up if evaluated by a younger brother. John was very human, slanting the story in favor of himself whenever he could. Although he was quite young when his father died, he must have known of the many times Edwin was pressed into appearing on stage to assume the role that his father, Junius Brutus Booth, should have played had he not been intoxicated. Young Edwin substituted many times, often before angry and abusive audiences who resented that they had paid to see the famous veteran actor and saw instead the young and often unprepared son, Edwin. One cannot study the life of Edwin Booth without feeling pity for the young actor who endured such trials during his formative years.

John's attitude toward his brother mellowed as time went on, but I found this difficult to understand. With a clearer insight into the personality of Edwin, my own sympathy for him waned.

9
BACKGROUND OF JOHN WILKES BOOTH

WHEN JOHN WAS JUST A BOY IN SCHOOL, A GYPSY IN A near-by wood read his palm and muttered, "Ah-h! You've a bad hand, the lines all cris-cras! It's full enough of sorrow—full of trouble—trouble in plenty. You'll break hearts, they'll be nothing to you. You'll die young, and leave many to mourn you. You'll make a bad end, and have plenty to love you. You'll have a fast life— short, but a grand one. Young sir, I've never seen a worse hand, and I wish I hadn't seen it, but if I were a girl I'd follow you through the world for your handsome face." (Quoted from *The Unlocked Book*.)

Born in Harford County, Maryland, in 1838, John Wilkes Booth was the son of Junius Brutus Booth, a great British tragedian, well-known for his Shakespearian roles on both the English and the American stage. The elder Booth met and fell in love with Mary Ann Holmes, a flower girl from the streets of London. Although married and the father of a son, Booth abandoned his family and, with his young mistress, emigrated to America.

Records show that the lovers stayed for a while in Calais, France, an interesting sidelight in view of the important part Calais was to play later in John's life. I could find no reason for this sojourn in France. The Booth males, it seems, had a fatal fascination for the opposite sex, and a habit of getting their love lives into hopeless tangles.

On June 30, 1821, Junius Brutus Booth and his then common-law wife, Mary Ann, landed in Norfolk, Virginia. They settled on a farm near Belair, Maryland, where their first child, Junius Brutus Booth Jr., was born. Nine of the Booth's ten children were born on the farm: on July 5, 1823, Rosalie was born. Ten years later came Edwin, born November 13, 1833, followed on November 19, 1835, by a sister, Asia, so named by her father because that was the continent where man first walked with God. John Wilkes was born May 10, 1838. The youngest child, Joseph Adrian, was born February 8, 1840. Little is known of the other children: Frederick, Elizabeth and Mary Ann, who died in infancy; and Henry, of small pox, aged eleven.

By the time John Wilkes was born, it was evident that the elder Booth suffered from a mental derangement which erupted from time to time in erratic behavior. In spite of his affliction, Junius Brutus Booth was a kind and gentle man. He was opposed to taking life, and forbade the eating of meat at his table.

John Wilkes, called "Johnny" during his childhood years, was badly spoiled. He was a strikingly beautiful child, with flashing black eyes and black, curly hair. A favorite of his father, loved and adored by his mother, he was a happy, carefree youngster given to pranks and occasional acts of rebellion, lightly tossed aside by his overly indulgent parents. The responsibility for his rearing fell to his mother because his actor-father was away from home for long periods of time. The boy was only thirteen when his father died.

John loved horses and learned to ride at an early age, but he was not known as an animal lover. He hated cats, and was reported to have killed all the cats on the farm in a fit of rage, to the horror of his nonviolent father,

During the course of the regressions, it was not difficult for me to take Booth back to his childhood and to hear his young voice recounting experiences similar to those of children everywhere. There was one exception.

Johnny had a fear of growing up. His childish voice tinged with the tone of a badly spoiled youngster would, at times, cry out, "I don't want to grow up! I want to stay the way I am!"

John had been a capricious youngster who often flung himself down upon the rich moist earth to smell, as he put it, "her sweet breath." He sang to the sunshine, loved to wander through the woods and feel the closeness of nature. All this was part of the man who coldbloodedly shot Abraham Lincoln to death in Ford's Theatre on April 14, 1865. John would have been twenty-seven on May 10—the first day of the conspiracy trial.

Step by step, I felt myself being drawn deeper into the whirlpool of mystery surrounding the life of John Wilkes Booth. It began to absorb my whole day, and at times intrude upon my dreams with such clarity that it became frightening.

The shadow of another world continued to cling to my work, but as time went on, countless experiences shattered any doubts I had of being able to communicate with that world. It is not easy to work on a case like Booth's; I found myself beginning to lead a twilight existence between one world and another, the boundary with reality becoming only an indistinct line.

I feel certain that as man reaches out to explore the

horizons of his mind and learns to go beyond his assumed limitations, he will find truths now outside the frontiers of his imagination. We have built fences with our minds, and are conditioned to be earthbound in our thinking, unable to comprehend limitless creativity—or God.

10
RELIVING THE ASSASSINATION

THE POET, WALT WHITMAN, WHO WROTE *O Captain! My Captain!* as a tribute to Abraham Lincoln, is said to have been in the theatre audience the night of the President's assassination, and to have written of the crime: ". . . the actual murder transpired with the quiet and simplicity of any commonest occurrence—the bursting of a bud or pod in the growth of vegetation. . . . Through the general hum following the stage pause, with the change of positions . . . came the muffled sound of a pistol shot, which not one-hundredth part of the audience heard. . . . "

After almost a year of regressions, I decided that the time had come to subject Booth to the ordeal of remembering the assassination. Perhaps then he would solve the mysteries surrounding the scene and tell me the plan that had enabled him to kill a president and safely make his way out of the country. The out-of-life state had been only partially successful. While Booth had talked, his conversation had been stilted and I was convinced that he was deliberately evading the climax of his story.

A certain amount of cowardice on my part contributed to the delay, for I was not looking forward to putting Booth through the ordeal. I had learned to like John after probing for many hours into his private life. In many ways he was a loving and warm personality, responding kindly and often gently. I was convinced that the assassination, for whatever reason, had not been a casual act. When Booth said that he had not regretted killing Lincoln, it was hard to believe he was telling the whole truth.

It was fortunate that, at that time, Doctor Hubert H. Case, my former instructor and longtime friend, decided to pay us a visit. Dr. Case is a well-known West Coast hypnotist with many years of experience in hypnotherapy. He has worked extensively with prebirth regressions, and when he consented to take Booth through the assassination, I was relieved.

I had grown too close to Booth, and was afraid I might lose my objectivity if I led him through the actual scene of the assassination. I didn't want to make any mistakes that could be avoided, and certainly believed that putting Wesley through such a traumatic experience should not be repeated.

With Wesley, I had used a technique known as "blocking"—giving a subject the suggestion that he not allow someone else to hypnotize him. This is not a technique I approve of for most subjects because it allows the hypnotist too much control and infringes upon the subject's free will. In Wesley's case, however, "blocking" seemed justified because it offered protection to him as well as to me.

Knowing that many others were aware of the work I was doing, there was an outside chance that someone might try to experiment with Wesley; the hours under hypnosis had made him very susceptible. I blocked him only in the realm of Booth's life—in other words, he could be hypnotized by anyone else, but the Booth life could not be reached. It is easy for the hypnotist to lift a block and allow another hypnotist to take over, but Dr. Case, when he learned that Wesley had been blocked, decided to try to break this barrier himself, to test the effectiveness of the technique.

Dr. Case worked for some time before he succeeded in bypassing the "block" and I was satisfied that this could not have been accomplished by an amateur. Once he had Wesley into the Booth life, Dr. Case began the regression:

Q. You are in the year of 1860, tell me, what year is it?
A. (*silence*)
Q. You can see a calendar, what is the year?
A. If I can see a calendar . . . why can't you?
Q. Because I am blind.
A. It's 1860 . . . of course!
Q. What is your name?
A. John! Do you know that there are times when you make absolutely no sense at all?
Q. Your name is John . . . What?
A. (*angry*) John Wilkes Booth! And what is your name . . . or have you changed it recently?
Q. You tell me, what is my name?
A. It is strange that you suddenly do not know your name.
Q. You are acting very snobbish and arrogant—whom do you think you are talking *to*?
A. And to WHOM DO YOU presume to be talking . . . sir? [Booth had become very angry and there was no point in continuing to argue with him.]
Q. It is now 1861; whom are you talking to?
A. Davy. [Because he was unfamiliar with the Booth history, Dr. Case did not know who Davy was and therefore did not question him about it.] We are moving ahead and it is 1862; how have you been feeling?

A. I have been feeling rather well.

Q. Now, we are moving into 1864. Tell me, have you any close friends?

A. I consider no one to be a really close friend.

Q. You do *not* have a close friend?

A. I find very few . . . actually there seems to be no one who is able to keep trust for a period of time . . . I find that they all betray the trust in one way or another . . . there is always something, money . . . position or greed.

Q. It must be very lonely for you.

A. Oh, I have people whom I acquaint myself with . . . people I socialize with . . . these people I find to be amusing for short periods of time . . . they distract my mind from any loneliness I might feel.

Q. Have you any business associates outside the theatre?

A. I have no business associates whatsoever in the theatre.

Q. All right, we are moving ahead to 1865, how is your cough?

A. Right now it is not bothering me . . . but it has been worse during the past few weeks.

Q. I understand that you are playing in the Ford's Theatre.

A. I have in the past and I will again . . . shortly.

Q. Are you looking forward to it?

A. As much as anyone could . . . playing in Washington. It should be a rather interesting performance.

Q. All right, we are going into Ford's Theatre, what are you going to do?

At this point Booth became very restless and upset, and again we saw something happen that neither Dr. Case nor I had ever seen before. Booth took himself backward in time and insisted that it was 1863. It was obvious that he was avoiding the assassination. Dr. Case, after several unsuccessful attempts to get him to enter into the scene

74

of the assassination, finally lost patience and used a direct approach.

Q. You are now entering the President's Box, what are you going to do?

A. (*Booth slowly reaches out and turns an imaginary doorknob, evidently the door to the President's Box. He slowly raises his right arm, pointing an imaginary gun downward, as though taking precise aim at a seated person. He squeezes the imagined trigger. His expression is deathlike, his movements slow and mechanical.*)

I felt a strange sickness well up inside me, making a slow journey to my throat, but I stood transfixed, unable to pull my eyes away from the moment of horror frozen for so long in history, being re-enacted here in my living room—John Wilkes Booth murdering President Lincoln. I felt the sting of hot tears blind my eyes. Incredible!

Q. You have fired the gun, now what are you doing?

A. (*Booth breathes heavily and grips his right leg, grimacing with pain.*)

Q. You have no physical pain at all.

A. It hurts!

Q. What hurts?

A. (*puzzled*) Something happened!

Q. What has happened?

A. I've been . . . shot!

Q. Where?

A. (*voice rising to near hysteria, Booth holds up his right leg*) In the leg . . . can't you see it? [According to history, Booth broke a small bone in his *left* ankle when he jumped to the stage.]

Q. Don't you think that you should get help?

A. (*voice under control*) If I can . . . just make it to the carriage . . . I will be all right.

Q. Where are you going?

A. To . . . Doctor Carter.

Q. Is he very far away?

A. Only . . . a few blocks.

Q. Now, you have arrived at Dr. Carter's, tell me what is going on.

A. Mr. Richards is helping me out of the carriage . . . into the building.

Q. And now what is happening?

A. (*Booth suddenly jerks his body upright and grips the arms of the chair; an agonizing gasp of pain escapes his lips*)

Q. What has happened?

A. (*the skin around the lips turns white, he draws his breath in another gasp of pain*)

Q. Why are you gasping, John?

A. (*gasps once more and perspiration forms on his brow; face grows pale and still, harsh lines of pain disappear as he seems to lose consciousness*)

Q. All right, I want you to rest now. The pain has gone and when I talk to you again, it will be the same time and the same place.

Q. (*a few minutes later*) Now, you know what you have done, are you excited?

A. (*Booth puts his hands over his ears, rocks back and forth, screams tearing from his throat*) NO! . . . NO! . . NO! (*tears flow down his cheeks from beneath his closed eyelids, dropping from his chin onto his shirt, wetting it; violent sobs rack his body*).

The sound of Booth's screams was heart-rending. Sobbing uncontrollably, I ran from the room, crying, "Oh, God, what have I done?" The screams followed me and echoed against the walls. I could hear also the quiet impersonal voice of Dr. Case as he demanded, "Why are you screaming?"

At last the house grew still. The screams subsided as Dr. Case brought Wesley out of hypnosis. Wesley seemed confused.

"Why am I all wet?" he asked. He felt his shirt front and took out a handkerchief to wipe his face—he looked exhausted. The regression had taken more than an hour; Wesley walked over to the couch and lay down.

"I am very tired," he said. I did not waken him until the following morning, when he told me that he felt fine, and seemed not to have suffered ill effects from the ordeal of the night before.

A few days later Wesley expressed a desire to hear the tape of the assassination, but as he listened he became very withdrawn. When I pressed for a reason, he told me that listening to the tape caused a number of jumbled pictures to come into his mind and, although the pictures made no sense to him, they had a very depressing effect. I immediately stopped the recorder, and Wesley has never heard the remainder of the assassination tape.

I had hoped that this regression would solve the mystery of what happened after the assassination of President Lincoln, but instead it left us with many unanswered questions: If Booth had been shot, who was his assailant? Who was Dr. Carter? What part had Mr. Richards played in the plot, or in the crime? Had his only job been to help Booth escape to the Garrett farm? Who *was* Mr. Richards?

We would have to wait for answers, because Dr. Case agreed with me that it would be unwise to subject Wesley to further questioning relating directly to the assassination so soon after allowing him to experience the trauma of remembering the crime. Meanwhile I turned my attention to the organization that played such an important part in Booth's life—The Knights of the Golden Circle.

11
THE KNIGHTS OF THE GOLDEN CIRCLE

MY FIRST THOUGHT, WHEN I HEARD OF THE SOCIETY OF men who called themselves The Knights of the Golden Circle, was that the name had a pleasant musical sound, but if the records of this secret society can be relied on, its name belied its purpose. C. A. Bridges describes it as follows:

When first organized, the association is said to have had rather ambitions plans and objectives. The idea and name, Golden Circle, came from the proposal that, with Havana as a center and a radius of sixteen geographical degrees or about 1,200 miles, a great circle be drawn that would include Maryland, Kentucky, southern Missouri, all the states south of them, a portion of Kansas, most of Texas and Old Mexico, all of Central America, the northern part of South America, and the entire West Indies. This area they proposed to unite into a gigantic slave empire that would rival in power and prestige the Roman Empire of two thousand years ago. Within this dream empire were the regions that produced nearly all of the world's supply of tobacco, cotton, sugar, and much of its finest rice and coffee. With a virtual world monopoly of these important commodities, it would have been, in fact, a rich region, stretching around the Gulf of Mexico like a great golden circle.

This alleged filibustering association is believed to have been organized and inspired by George Bickley in the late 1850s, and to have had two main objectives: to foster and protect Southern rights, and to annex parts of Mexico to the Southern slave empire. If Booth was a member of such an organization, the extent of his activities is not known.

Under regression, Booth claimed that to reveal any activity, or a member's name, to anyone outside the Circle (he always referred to the society as the "Circle"), meant certain death, but because he had "returned from the grave," and no longer feared reprisal, he answered my questions freely.

Q. What kind of oath did you take to become a member of the Circle?
A. Mostly concerning secrecy . . . very simple.
Q. What was the punishment for violation of the oath?
A. Death!
Q. Were there many who violated the oath?
A. No!
Q. Can you think of anyone who did?
A. No one ever talked enough to do . . . more than . . . get himself . . . killed.
Q. Can you tell me where The Knights of the Golden Circle got its name?
A. I am not certain . . . the organization to which I . . . originally belonged . . . got its name from a

previous organization . . . that had pretty much died out.

Q. Were they organized in the South to begin with?

A. No.

Q. Did it start around Washington?

A. No.

Q. Where did it start?

A. Originally . . . it started in Albany.

Q. Who, in Albany, started it?

A. Just . . . a group of business men I was . . . acquainted with.

Q. How did they come to accept you?

A. It was a matter of being recommended . . . by several people . . . and being voted on.

Q. Were there some well-known figures in the Circle?

A. Some were prominent in social and business . . . there were others . . .

Q. Who were some of them?

A. Andrew Johnson was one . . . Senator Hale . . . Mr. Benjamin . . .

Q. Who was Mr. Benjamin . . . what did he do?

A. He was a well-known banker.

Q. And Senator Hale was a member?

A. Yes. [As I questioned Booth, it was surprising to learn of his abiding friendship for Senator John Parker Hale from New Hampshire—contradicting history.]

Q. John, tell me about Senator Hale.

A. He was a quiet man . . . concerned for the future of his country . . . upset with the discord . . . the war. He wanted peace and happiness for all mankind.

Q. Was Senator Hale against slavery?

A. Openly, yes. . . . There weren't many of us for slavery . . . the enslavement of fellow human beings . . . is not very nice.

Q. On the day of the assassination, did you meet Senator Hale?

A. No . . . met the evening before . . . two occasions.

Q. Where?

A. His study and small . . . (*fades*).

Q. Did he have an appointment with President Lincoln?

A. A dinner appointment . . . met later in office . . . or small room . . . small parlor or anteroom . . . can't place location.

Q. What about Senator Hale's daughter, Bessie? [Her photograph, and those of four other women, was found with Booth's diary on the body of the man who died at the Garrett farm.]

A. She was an attractive young woman . . . I used to escort her on occasion. . . . I have heard she was infatuated with me . . . but I don't believe this. Actors have a reputation . . . and no matter how good they are . . . or how well-received . . . it is not considered a very high . . . what word shall I use . . . station? . . . to be seen with an actor, escorted by one. Well . . . this was Senator Hale's excuse for pretending to dislike me . . . Bessie knew nothing of her father's involvement in the Circle . . . but I think she knew that she was being used . . . and that there was a good reason for it. . . . She never questioned.

Q. Did she know of your escape after the assassination? [It is a matter of record that Bessie Hale, although closely associated with Booth, was never subjected to intensive questioning after the assassination, and within a few weeks Hale and his family had sailed for Spain where he had been appointed Ambassador.]

A. There would have been no reason . . . for her to have known.

Q. You weren't above using a woman, were you John?

A. I wasn't above using anyone if it was necessary . . . but not for myself . . . and I can't remember ever using someone if it would cause harm to that person . . . not if there were some other way.

Booth made a sharp distinction between members of the Circle and workers who were hired to do a job, but who knew nothing about the inner workings of the organization. The Circle operated in echelon as a security measure, and to guard against exposure. Should any member or worker be caught, he could tell only what he knew at his own level.

Q. Who introduced you to the Circle?
A. My older brother . . . Junius. Actually he didn't introduce me to the Circle . . . but he was very instrumental . . . in introducing me.
Q. Did he continue in the Circle?
A. For a while . . . until it became extremely active. . . . I don't know that he resigned . . . but he was not included in plans. . . . Now, another group thought . . . the Circle should be . . . mystic . . . should have rituals . . . costumes . . . high priests . . . and all of that . . . and this also served a purpose. They were patted on the back . . . and allowed to do the things they wished. They became the public image . . . or the play that the public saw . . . but like a play . . . there were things going on . . . backstage . . .
Q. What was the purpose of the Circle?
A. Originally . . . it was just a meeting of men of similar interests . . . later became an organization to address problems of a particular time . . . later . . . to act on problems of the time . . . we did whatever we considered necessary. . . . Eventually we remedied many problems . . . many injustices . . . not only politically, but privately.

Q. Where did the Circle hold meetings?
A. Sometimes in private homes . . . sometimes in . . . offices. It depended . . . different places . . . in different areas.
Q. Who was head of The Knights of the Golden Circle?
A. I was . . . for a long time.

According to Booth, as the Circle grew it reached out to embrace other nations, and there began to be changes. He never said who initiated the changes. Perhaps he didn't know.

Q. Were the goals of the Circle in other countries the goals of the Circle in America?
A. The Circle always maintained the same basic goals . . . ideals . . . and concepts. . . . Unity . . . . . . stability . . . for one thing. . . . Economic stability was needed in each individual country . . . political stability also . . . then social . . . and finally . . . religious. This could be accomplished . . . by placing . . . certain people in power in each country. . . . This would bring about . . . change.
Q. Did you have a superior to whom you reported?
A. There was a small group that included Stanton . . . Seward . . . Johnson . . . and another . . . but I can't recall his name . . . but there wasn't any one of us . . . superior to the other.
Q. What was the password for The Knights of the Golden Circle?
A. It varied from time to time.
Q. What was the usual password that was used?
A. (silence)
Q. You didn't come right out and ask, "Are you a member of the Circle?"—or did you?
A. We all had code names . . . usually some part of

our name that was not commonly known . . . perhaps a middle name . . . perhaps a shortened version of the last name. . . . It varied from person to person. . . . A code name was used . . . but if we saw each other on a walkway we would not recognize each other . . . unless . . . of course . . the situation demanded it.

Q. What were you called in the Circle?

A. The majority of the time . . . Wilkes . . sometimes . . . John . . . but that was unusual.

Q. John, what name did you call Stanton within the Circle?

A. Masters. [Booth finally had provided the source of the name he had written during an earlier regression: Stanton's full name was *Edwin McMasters Stanton!*]

12
A POSTMORTEM

THE STORY OF PRESIDENT LINCOLN'S ASSASSINATION came through the lips of Wesley in the strange, theatrical voice of Booth. His vivid description of what happened that night at Ford's Theatre is rich with memories of another time, and very different from recorded history. Dr. Case had *confronted* Booth with his crime—this regression was conducted in the *out-of-life* state.

Q. John, I want you to tell me what you remember about killing President Lincoln.
A. I remember entering the box . . . and leaping from it . . . but I don't remember . . . anything at all . . . in between.
Q. Are you certain that you did the killing?
A. Of course! I know that I did it . . . I just don't remember . . . doing it.
Q. John, were you carrying a knife?
A. No . . . I don't think so.

87

Q. Did Major Rathbone try to stop you from killing the President?

A. *(no answer)*

Q. Did you knife Major Rathbone in the box?

A. I don't think so . . . but then again . . . I might have . . . I just don't remember. [It has been recorded that after shooting President Lincoln, Booth stabbed Major Rathbone who, with his fiancée, was a guest in the Presidential box the night of the assassination. The Major had jumped up to grapple with Booth, but the assassin managed to shake him off and, brandishing a knife, leapt to the stage with the cry, *"Sic semper tyrannis!"*—"Thus always to tyrants!"—the motto of Virginia.]

Q. All right, let's go back for a moment. How did you know President Lincoln would attend the theatre that night?

A. It was prearranged by his private staff.

Q. How far in advance did you know?

A. . . . No positive way of telling . . . we were all fairly certain a week before. . . . Things were done to . . . give the impression . . . that it was proper . . . for the President to attend . . . he went right along.

Q. Did it take you a long time to make up your mind to kill President Lincoln?

A. I wasn't completely sure . . . that I was going to . . . kill him . . . until I entered the box . . . I had a weapon with me . . . [According to history, Booth had decided only that day to kill the President.]

Q. Were you afraid that you lacked the nerve?

A. It was not a question of nerve! . . . But up until I reached the box . . . I kept wondering . . . I kept thinking of all the ways it might be done . . . was this . . . the right way? . . . Finally I decided that it had . . . to be done . . . I . . . *(voice breaking on last words)* . . . shot Mr. Lincoln! . . . *(appears to be entering into direct scene of assassination.)*

Q. John, you are not living—you are only remembering back. There is no reason to be upset. You are only relating what took place many years ago. [I allowed him a moment's rest before continuing.] All right, now I want you to tell me everything that happened at Ford's Theatre that night. You are not there, but you are able to see it and it does not upset you in any way. You have just leapt from the box and have landed on the stage; are you hurt?

A. No . . . I performed a pratfall.

A. What are you doing now?

A. I get up and limp across the length of the stage . . . I go backstage and open the door. . . . Something happens!

Q. What has happened, John?

A. I've been shot! *(breathing heavily and talking to himself)* I must close the door . . .

Q. All right, the door is closed, what are you doing?

A. Mr. Richards is helping me into the carriage.

Q. Where are you going?

A. I must get to Dr. Carter . . . it is not far . . .

Q. Do you know who shot you?

A. No.

Q. From what direction did you leave Washington?

A. Southeast.

Q. Did you cross the Navy Yard Bridge?

A. No . . . we crossed by boat.

Q. Did you manage to get the carriage across?

A. No, there was another one waiting on the other side . . . a short distance from the landing.

Q. Where were you going?

A. The destination was the farm.

Q. Were you acquainted with people on the farm?

A. The Garretts?

Q. Yes.

A. No . . . I had never met them.

Q. Did you meet Davy and Brown at the farm?

A. Oh no, I had to leave before they arrived.

Q. Why did you miss meeting them?

A. I don't know . . . what happened . . . they didn't make it in time and I had to leave. I couldn't wait any longer.

Q. I want you to be very explicit in answering my next question: How did you protect yourself against the possibility of the Circle killing you, once you had shot President Lincoln?

A. I knew they wanted to kill me . . . just as I knew they wanted to kill Johnson . . . it would hasten their claim to power. . . . They had designated a particular person . . . to make the attempt on my life . . . he had come to me . . . and I made him aware that . . . if I died by his hands . . . the entire Circle—all those involved in the conspiracy against Lincoln—would be revealed to the American people.

Booth also described a code devised to protect him from those members of the Circle who wanted him out of the way after he had killed Lincoln. Three men who were loyal to Booth received twelve pieces of coded paper with orders to forward them to a fourth man, Richards, should Booth be killed before he reached England. Mr. Richards, the man who had helped Booth escape, would know what to do if he was murdered.

I questioned Booth again about what happened after he had stumbled to his feet on stage and was making his way to the stage door. He said he expected to be fired at—"the man was an excellent marksman"—but he had no choice; (*with a wry smile*) "I couldn't very well stay in the theatre." What galled Booth was that he had been running—"If I had hesitated for a moment . . . I might only have been grazed."

I questioned Booth about what happened after he left the theatre.

Q. How did it happen that someone was mistaken for you?

A. It was a prearranged plan . . . a double was hired . . . an actor named Brown . . . I had worked with him in New York . . . he drank heavily . . . was always in need of money. . . . When the Circle approached him with an offer of five thousand dollars . . . he agreed. Brown didn't know how much to ask . . . besides . . . he was assured that the job wouldn't be too dangerous.

The play that night at Ford's Theatre was a comedy, "Our American Cousin," and Booth chose carefully the moment for his crime, when only one character would be on stage; his cue was a line from the second scene of the third act, when the character, Trenchard, soliloquizes, "Don't know the manners of good society, eh? Well, I guess I know enough to turn you inside out, old gal—you sockdologizing old man trap!"

Brown, according to Booth, was to stand outside a window, and listen for the line of the play that was the signal for him to mount his horse, and be ready to gallop off when Booth opened the door to the alley and jumped into the carriage with Mr. Richards.

Brown's instructions were to ride to the Navy Yard Bridge and call out the name, "Booth," to gain permission to cross. Davy Herold, Booth's accomplice, had orders to wait for a few minutes; then ride to the bridge to follow Brown. The two fugitives were to cross the bridge separately and meet a few miles from town; from there they would ride together to Surratt's Tavern to pick up a package and a bottle of whiskey. According to the plan,

Booth said, Brown was to stay with his horse, and only Davy enter the tavern, but they were to make every effort to be seen—and remembered—later.

Q. What was to become of the decoy, Brown, when he reached the Garrett farm—was he to leave the farm in another direction?

A. Richards was going to kill him.

Q. Why?

A. As long as he remained alive . . . I was not safe. He knew too much.

Q. Now, John, what about the diary? How did it happen to be on the body of Brown?

A. It was given to Davy . . . if Davy felt that it was necessary for positive identification.

Q. Had you written something in the diary?

A. Some of the writing was mine. [Stanton impounded Booth's diary for two years after the assassination; when it was released, eighteen pages were missing.]

Q. John, in the diary there is a statement: "I have almost a mind to return to Washington and . . . clear my name, which I feel I can do." Was this something you had written?

A. No . . . at the time of the assassination . . . and after . . . I had no intention of staying in Washington . . . or the United States . . .

Q. Have you any idea who could have written in your diary to make it sound like you?

A. . . . The diary at the farm . . . was partly written by me. Other parts, I was later informed . . . I had not written. [When Secretary Stanton surrendered Booth's diary to a Congressional Committee, he denied any knowledge of the missing pages; claimed that he had only seen it as presented. Parts of the diary, Booth said, had not been in his style. Certainly the few letters I obtained from the Archives that had been written by Booth bore his statement out. He was not "flowery" in speech or in writing. In doing handwriting comparisons, I found that in a few of the earlier books regarding the assassination, the Archive document—supposedly Booth's diary—varied, not only in handwriting, but in actual wording from the same document in later books. There seems to be no explanation as to how this happened.]

When I asked Booth what he had hoped to gain by killing President Lincoln, he denied any bid for personal acclaim, saying that one of the reasons for the assassination was the Circle's strong opposition to the President's stand on the economic fate of the South: "It was almost as if he [Lincoln] believed that the way to improve the South economically was to devastate it completely. We [the Circle] wanted to see the South . . . and the whole country . . . back on its feet, standing together . . . economically sound."

Booth believed that Lincoln had used the slaves as a political foil and Southerners resented this: "The South's bitterness toward the North could not be changed overnight, nor has it changed during the last few years. And—from what I have heard—I am not certain that it will ever change."

I questioned Booth once more about the assassination:

Q. John, you were not really a killer—this must have been very hard for you to live with?
A. I thought about it on occasion . . . but the act had to be done.
Q. That is true, you couldn't erase it and you couldn't go back, could you?
A. (*lines of suffering deepen in his face*) I knew . . . even on my way across country . . . that it had been done . . . President Lincoln . . . was dead . . . there was nothing I could do . . . I had to go on . . . I just had to force it out of my mind . . . force myself to forget it. . . . There were

other things I had to do . . . to create a whole new life for myself . . . and continue.

Q. Looking back, John, do you believe that you did the right thing?

A. I cannot say . . . that the death of Lincoln . . . was a mistake. . . . One thing . . . still upsetting . . . is that . . . people who are (*unclear*) in the assassination . . . became so corrupt . . . and ended with so much power.

13
CONSPIRACY WITHIN THE CIRCLE

I WAS DETERMINED TO TRY TO LEARN THE TRUE IDENTITY of Mr. Richards, the man Booth said waited in the carriage for him when he escaped from the theatre after the assassination. He had given me the name of "Nelson," and on information which I had gathered, I questioned him about it.

Although I was to learn later that "Nelson" was just another assumed name for Richards, the regression provided more clues to the mysterious and clandestine activities of The Knights of the Golden Circle.

Q. What was the first name of Mr. Richards?
A. Richard.
Q. Was he related to anyone you knew?
A. What do you mean, "Related to anyone I knew?" I knew him.
Q. Did you know any of his relatives?
A. I am not certain that I did, no.

95

Q. Wasn't one of Davy's sisters married to a man named Nelson?

A. I am not certain.

Q. Was there any relationship between Richards and Davy?

A. (*with acerbity*) None that I knew of. . . . Perhaps there could have been . . . his family was his affair. I didn't intrude in the private lives of Circle members, and I tried to avoid socializing except at business meetings. . . . If I was invited to social gatherings that included other Circle members, I declined . . . I believed this was the best way to avoid suspicion. I did not believe that socializing for its own sake was in the best interest of the Circle . . . of the movement . . . of the cause, or for that matter, anyone's private welfare. . . . It could upset the delicate balance between what was supposed to be known and what *was* known.

During this regression Booth admitted that after the assassination he and Richards had traveled to the Garrett farm, and that Richards was to have killed the decoy Brown if he had been there. Davy Herold, who was hanged for his part in the conspiracy, was expected to accompany Booth from the farm to San Francisco.

Q. Was Davy Herold mentally retarded?

A. (*puzzled*) I . . . I don't . . .

Q. Did he use his head, could he think well?

A. I had not thought that he could think as well as I . . . he wasn't nearly as educated . . . but he wasn't . . . crazy.

Q. No, but would you have described him as dull-witted?

A. To some extent, yes . . . not as much as some . . . he knew what to do. We had been over the plans several times and he knew them quite well. . . . Davy was not one to panic . . . to become upset and forget . . . as many might have done. He fully understood the route and the rest of it . . . and as I have said before . . . I really don't know what happened. He was able to do many things by himself . . . and without any help or previous discussion. That was one of the reasons why I wanted him to come to San Francisco with me . . . I knew what work was needed there . . . and I knew that Davy could manage it. Apart from that, he would have been removed from Washington . . . and far enough away not to be . . . bothered by anyone.

Q. Many people were used in the conspiracy, weren't they?

A. Yes . . . but the times that harm came to them was when they had not completed the task assigned.

A. I wouldn't think that would apply necessarily to Davy. He ran into some unforeseen situations, didn't he?

A. To an extent . . . that is true. If he had run into any difficulty . . . and was unable to make proper connections . . . at the farm . . . at the appointed time . . . if there was any reason to believe that things were going wrong . . . there was an alternate plan he could have executed. I waited at the farm for as long as possible . . . then I had to leave. . . . I left with the hope that if Davy had encountered some difficulty . . . he would have chosen the second plan . . . and carried on from there. . . . I found out later that this was not true.

Q. What was the alternate plan?

A. Davy had been told that after leaving Dr. Mudd's house . . . if there was a delay . . . there was another place where he could go . . . a place owned by a man named Stewart . . . closer than the Garrett farm . . . and a little to the west. The second plan was similar to the first. . . . If nothing was found at the Garrett farm . . . then as an alternative . . . the authorities would have been given orders to search the vicinity of the Stewart place. . . . This would have given Davy an additional day in which to find . . . and dispose of Booth's impersonator, and be on his way. I don't know what happened to him.

I could find historical record of three Stewarts: a Dr. Richard Stewart, who gave Booth and Herold a meal but would not let them spend the night at his house, and who refused to examine Booth's injured leg; Joseph B. Stewart, a Washington lawyer who had been in the audience when Lincoln was shot, and who positively identified Booth as the assassin, and Edward C. Stewart, telegraph operator at the Metropolitan Hotel, which Booth was known to have frequented.

If it is true that the Garretts were not at the farm when the *real* Booth arrived, they did not see John Wilkes Booth, but saw the impostor instead. According to Booth, the Circle had paid Garrett to take his family and leave the farm for a few hours. They were not told why the farm was needed, and when questioned later, were paid to keep quiet. Their testimony that Booth and Davy had come to their farm was true. The two desperate men were traveling under assumed names and it is unlikely that the Garretts suspected anything at first.

The Circle protected itself by using people, giving money when necessary, for silence or favors. The Garretts could not tell what they did not know, so there was no danger that their story would be discredited.

Four, including Davy Herold, were charged with conspiracy in connection with the assassination and sentenced to death, but each knew only his or her own role. In the next regression Booth explained how these four paid with their lives on the gallows for being linked to the crime.

14
FOUR WHO WERE HANGED AS CONSPIRATORS

MARY SURRATT, THE WIDOW WHO RAN THE WASHINGTON boarding house where Booth stayed, was the first woman in this country to be executed for a "crime," and one of four persons charged with conspiracy and hanged following the assassination of President Lincoln.

The others were: George Atzerodt, Davy Herold, and Lewis Paine. Booth tells about the four, as he knew them.

Q. Of the four who were hanged as conspirators, what about Davy Herold? Why wasn't his life spared?

[Twenty-two-year-old David Herold was described by friendly witnesses at the conspiracy trial as being something of an imbecile; pleasant, trifling, but irresponsible.]

A. I don't know . . . he was to have been saved . . . to have been imprisoned and later released . . . something went wrong . . . I never knew for certain. I was sorry Davy had to be hanged . . . he played a small part. . . . Others actually played no part . . . so far as the total conspiracy was concerned . . . they were only laborers . . . only working for a living. . . . As far as conspiracy planning details . . . they only did what they were told to do.

Q. Did any belong to the Circle?

A. No . . . they were hired by the Circle . . . others on trial were only connected in . . . a small way.

Q. What about Mrs. Surratt?

A. Mrs. Surratt . . . who was implicated . . . was aware . . . was really more a friend . . . a person I had become acquainted with. Her son was a part-time crook . . . I don't know what became of him. . . . Any blame he received was unfounded. Just the same . . . his ideals were very low. . . . He tried to play the . . . "man about town" . . . but unfortunately . . . he didn't like to spend his own money . . . he really wasn't capable of playing the part.

Q. Can you tell me about Dr. Mudd? [Dr. Samuel Alexander Mudd, according to history, was the doctor who set Booth's leg, broken when he caught his spur in the Treasury flag as he leapt from the Presidential box to the stage. Booth said his boot, found under a bed in the Mudd house and later produced as evidence that Booth had been treated by Dr. Mudd following the assassination, had been planted there a few days before the assassination, and that Davy Herold had purposefully broken the leg of the decoy after giving him drugged whiskey at Surratt's tavern. The false beard that the decoy tried to keep on his face, and that reportedly kept slipping down while he was being treated by Mudd, led me to question Booth as to how a beard might be attached to his face if he were playing a part where a beard was necessary. He told me that a beard was never put on in one piece but was glued on bit by bit, and the problem was not in keeping it in place, but in removing it.]

A. As for Dr. Mudd . . . prior to the assassination . . . he had found out certain information . . . which he was not to know . . . and threatened to use it against the Circle. . . . They warned him . . . decided to implicate him. [John Surratt and Dr. Samuel Mudd were not hanged for their suspected involvement. John Surratt escaped to Canada, then to Europe where he enlisted with the Vatican Zouaves. He was captured in Egypt in 1867, and shipped back on a naval vessel to the United States where he was tried and later released. Dr. Mudd was tried, convicted, and sentenced to hard labor in the military prison at Dry Tortugas, Florida. He was released, broken in health, in March, 1869.]

Q. What part did George from Port Tobacco play in this?

A. . . . George played really a very small part . . . not in the vicinity . . . nor around at the time. . . . Played large part in whole affair. . . . He was in charge of finances . . . was the one who provided the monies . . . that various people were paid . . . to do various actions. . . . I was paid from some monies he had gathered . . . mostly from people in the South . . . who were aware of the things we were trying to do . . . and were in favor of our actions. Because of his [George Atzerodt's] position . . . in Port Tobacco . . . it was easy for him to travel . . . he was a Southern sympathizer . . . rather influential . . . able to procure money more easily . . . than someone else. [It has been accepted as historical fact that George Atzerodt, the German-born carriage painter from Port Tobacco, was assigned to murder Vice-President Johnson. That cowardice prevented the would-be murderer from committing the crime was attested to by David

M. DeWitt, who writes that ". . . he . . . (At-zerodt) went no nearer his prey than the bar. . . . Poor, pitiable caricature of an assassin."]

Q. What about his attempt on Andrew Johnson's life?

A. I had taken care of his plans . . . made sure that they did not develop . . . I don't know what *he* expected to gain, unless perhaps an appointment . . . to some high-level post.

Q. Tell me about Lewis Paine.

A. I . . . I'm trying to think for a moment.

Q. Didn't he also use the name of Powell? [According to record, Paine was an alias for the accused conspirator, Lewis Thornton Powell.]

A. No . . . I was trying to remember about Mr. Paine . . . for one thing, he was a crook. He was in some ways—well, you might compare his livelihood with that of Mr. Richards. There was one difference . . . Mr. Richards was true to what he believed. Mr. Paine believed in nothing—favored no cause. He would take money from one person . . . to do a job . . . and turn right around and sell his services to a rival . . . for a little higher price . . . so that other person could, for instance . . . stay alive. I had no faith in Mr. Paine . . . and was not surprised that he was accused of attacking Mr. Seward . . . this was interesting, considering the job he had been paid to do.

Q. What was that?

A. To start a ruckus in the street outside Ford's Theatre . . . to divert people as I was leaving by the exit at the rear. There was a brawl just as the President was being removed from the theatre . . . but two others had been commissioned to start one in case Paine failed . . . he could never be trusted . . . that was the sort of man he was. Maybe he was paid to attack Seward . . . someone was to fake an attempt on his life . . . but Paine carried it too far. If Mr. Seward was the one who hired Paine, he must have been . . . shall we say . . . shocked? [Big, powerful Lewis Paine, an ex-Confederate soldier, made an attempt on the life of Secretary of State William H. Seward, viciously knifing him while he was in bed.]

Mr. Paine was often mistaken for Mr. Powell because the two men looked somewhat alike . . . it was sometimes difficult to tell where either was at a given time. But there the resemblance stopped . . . Mr. Powell was trustworthy . . . Paine was not!

15
A STRANGE DREAM

ONE NIGHT WESLEY HAD A DREAM ABOUT THE assassination. He awoke suddenly and the only thing he could remember was the name, "Forrest Parker." He wrote the name down so that I might question Booth about it.

Q. John, who was Forrest Parker?
A. Among other things . . . he was the man who shot me.

John Forrest Parker was hired by Mrs. Lincoln from the ranks of the Metropolitan Police Force—although his police record had been poor. Responsible for guarding the President's box on the night of the assassination, Parker left his post. What he did immediately after the assassination has not been definitely determined. In spite of this negligence, he was allowed to go free while many others were locked up, including John Ford who owned the theatre. Parker was not called upon to testify at the conspiracy trial.

I recalled that John Parker was the name of the guard posted to protect President Lincoln at Ford's Theatre, but I had not remembered a middle name.

Q. Who was he, and did he have any other purpose for being near the theatre that evening?

A. I was his purpose for being there. . . . He was also doing duty inside the theatre.

Q. Was his duty to guard the President?

A. Yes.

Q. Was he a Circle member?

A. He was probably one of the best shots in Washington . . . and he had been hired numerous times . . . by the Circle. . . . It had been decided by certain people who wished to do me harm . . . to hire him to attempt to kill me. . . . He didn't succeed . . . and this was because he was far more loyal to me for things I had done for him . . . on many occasions . . . than he was to those . . . who had approached him. . . . It was interesting that he was chosen to guard Lincoln. . . . I understood that later on . . . it was claimed by many . . . that it had been Mrs. Lincoln's decision . . . but . . . if so . . . I wonder who persuaded her?

Q. It couldn't have been Stanton, could it?

A. I really don't know . . . I have every reason to believe it was . . . and that he probably forced Mrs. Lincoln . . . in some way . . . probably in fear . . . for her own life.

In a letter dated March 15, 1866, the President's widow, Mary Todd Lincoln, wrote to her correspondent, a Mrs. Orme, "As sure as you and I live, Johnson had some hand in this." She expanded wanderingly on an imagined conspiracy between the assassin and President Johnson: "Why was that card of Booth's found in his box? . . . I have been deeply impressed with the harrowing thought that he had an understanding with the conspirators, and they knew their man."

While the widow of Abraham Lincoln mourned bitterly for her "sainted husband," the women who had loved John Wilkes Booth wept for the assassin. One of these women was the prostitute, Ella Turner Starr, who unsuccessfully tried to kill herself by swallowing chloroform. She lay down to die with Booth's picture under her pillow. When I questioned Booth about her, he answered candidly.

Q. John, who was Ella Starr?
A. There was a woman . . . I'm trying to place her. . . . She was a very nice woman . . . and I talked with her . . . on many occasions.
Q. You only talked with her?
A. *(smiling)* She was rather attractive.
Q. She must have been; I notice that you are smiling.
A. There were moments of pleasure we shared . . . she was a dear companion . . . one I could call upon. We were more than acquaintances.
Q. John, was Miss Starr a prostitute?
A. *(showing startled surprise, hesitating before answering)* . . . I suppose you would have to say that she was. . . . She could seduce any man . . . I am quite certain of that . . . but I always felt she offered me something more . . . when I simply needed a person to talk to . . . some quiet place for myself. . . . which proved—at least to me—that to her . . . I was someone special.
Q. Was she aware of your intent to assassinate President Lincoln?
A. No . . . I did not tell her of the plan . . . but she knew that I was involved with a secret organization . . . and she was helpful.
Q. Did she get some kind of information for you?
A. . . . Information that members of the Circle . . .

were going to make an attempt . . . on the life of Andrew Johnson . . . was probably the most significant. . . . Ella helped me . . . she knew the innuendos of her trade . . . Instructed me in the finer points of her profession. . . . I was as aware of the capabilities of these women . . . as they themselves were.

Q. The way you speak of women, you seem to know a great deal about them.

A. One needed to know.

Q. Yes, I suppose that's true. Now, let's return to Ella Starr—was there other information?

A. . . . Another time . . . she told me about a raid that would have been disastrous. . . . Ella was friendly with some of the military, who . . . being the sort of men they are . . . like to boast to their women . . . of their daring deeds.

Q. Who were some of the military men with whom Miss Starr had relations?

A. I didn't know all of them.

Q. Whom did you know?

A. I knew of one military man in particular . . . who proved helpful . . .

Q. Who was he?

A. I'm referring to General Grant.

Q. What can you tell me about him?

A. He was a drunken fool! . . . He had childish ways . . . and no capacity for reasoning . . . or thinking . . . other than killing.

Q. You paint quite a picture of him.

A. An accurate one! . . . When Ella met Grant . . . he was not active in the military . . . he was merely someone who had come to her for a certain amount of pleasure. . . . She was later to find out, as I did, that it was . . . useful for her to know him. . . . He was probably one of the most naive men in the military.

Q. Do you know why General Grant was not in the theatre the night you assassinated President Lincoln?

A. No . . . I can't remember whether he was to attend . . . or whether something happened to change his plans . . . I have heard that he was occupied with someone else.

Q. What were you going to do if General Grant had been in the box that evening? Would that have altered *your* plans?

A. No.

Q. Were you going to kill him too?

A. There would have been no reason to kill him.

Q. Was Grant a member of the Circle?

A. No.

Q. Now, there has been a great deal of speculation about General Grant, who had been scheduled to attend the theatre that evening—did Grant know that something was going to happen to Lincoln?

A. Oh . . . no!

Q. He wasn't part of the conspiracy?

A. No.

Q. And there was never any plan to assassinate General Grant?

A. Not to my knowledge . . . no . . . he had decided to be the successor to Johnson . . . in fact . . . Johnson himself . . . among others . . . had decided that . . . had made the decision not to spend more than one term there.

Q. Is it true that Stanton and Seward planned to kill Andrew Johnson?

A. And me . . . I was aware of it almost as soon as . . . the planning had begun. . . . I presented it to certain members of the Circle . . . not including Stanton or Seward.

Q. When Stanton died, it was said that he might have committed suicide, did you know about that?

A. *(vehemently)* Stanton would never have committed suicide!

Q. John, who was the most important person in the Circle—in England?

A. *(clearing his throat in an exaggerated manner and smiling)*

Q. Oh! I'm looking at him?

This remark of mine was off-guard. I completely confused Booth. He began to drift and his voice was weak, "I do not understand. . . ." Evidently he knew that I could not see him because he was unable to see me. He became so upset that I had to terminate the regression. After I brought Wesley around, he asked that I put him back into hypnosis as he felt fine and was sure that Booth would continue to talk. This was done, and we picked up where we had left off.

When I was trying to learn the true identity of "Mr. Benjamin," I worded another question badly, and spoiled the regression. I said, "John, I want you to think this over very carefully, because I wouldn't want to accuse the wrong man." Instantly, he turned on me, and when he spoke his voice was sharp with suspicion.

"Accuse!" he shot at me. "Accuse him of what?"

I was startled by his direct question, but realizing immediately what I had done, I tried to smooth over the situation. I assured him that I had unthinkingly used the wrong word. He seemed to accept this, but after a few brief sentences, he suddenly stopped and commented, "I still don't understand what it was that you wanted to accuse him of." I could not skirt his defensiveness, and had to terminate the regression.

Booth evaded truth more quickly than he lied deliberately. He was capable of weaving a falsehood—acting was his profession—but I became so in tune with him that in most instances I was able to detect by his expression and the tone of his voice when he was making an attempt to mislead me. When I challenged him on the grounds that I knew something about an incident that he had embellished, he would quickly back off with a weak remark such as, "Well, that was what I always told others."

Q. All right, John—now, the reasons behind the killing of President Lincoln have never been quite clear. I have been talking to you for a long time and I can't believe that you were actually a killer.

A. No . . . well . . . it would have been very simple to have hired someone else . . . it had been discussed . . . on several occasions . . . the hiring of someone . . . either within . . . or out of . . . the Circle.

Q. But why you, John?

A. Why not?

Q. I guess that is a good answer.

A. . . . No . . . what I thought in later years . . . was one thing . . . but what I thought at the time . . . [he was starting to mumble, but I did not press him.]

Q. I have wondered, John, when you lay in Calais with your life approaching an end, what did you really feel—what were your thoughts?

A. I wondered from time to time . . . before I died. . . . I wondered what were men's thoughts . . . when they . . . were close . . . to death. . . . Do they look back on their lives . . . and think . . . "Was it worth it?" . . . I don't know whether it was . . . worth it or not . . . only time will tell . . . only time . . . *(voice fading away).*

111

16
THE MYSTERIOUS DOCTOR CARTER

HAVING LIVED HIS LIFE IN THE SHADOW, WITH EVERY MOment guarded, Booth knew all the tricks of evasion and, with the release of death, still clung to what he considered "his own private business." The case of Dr. Carter was no exception.

At first Booth was reluctant to tell me much, but as in other instances, I found The Knights of the Golden Circle to be the key to the locked doors of his memory. For some time before asking these questions, I had been hammering questions at Booth regarding his Circle activities.

Q. How did Dr. Carter happen to be in Washington the night of the assassination?
A. He had been in town for several days.
Q. Where had he come from?
A. . . . From Richmond.
Q. What was he doing in Richmond?

A. Not certain . . . *(sarcastically)* I assume he was practicing his profession

Q. What was Dr. Carter's first name?

A. Charles.

Q. John, how much were you paid by the Circle to kill Lincoln? [I took a chance by asking this question, but it was not just a stab in the dark. Booth had given many indications that he had been paid, and by whom.]

A. Twenty-five thousand dollars.

Q. Who put the money together?

A. . . . Some from the South . . . don't know where it all came from.

Q. Who paid you?

A. Rich——Dr. Carter . . . when I arrived at the house with Mr. Richards . . . I found Dr. Carter . . . the money had been entrusted to him . . . as a safeguard . . . he would know what to do if anything . . . happened to me. . . . If I made it those few blocks, I would probably make it the . . . rest of the way [to the Garrett Farm] . . . but he knew . . . that if I was killed . . . he was to deposit the money in the bank . . . in Canada . . . where it would be used as needed . . . by those who had access to it.

Q. You said you were paid in full—what did you do with the money you received for killing Lincoln?

A. . . . Sent it to a bank.

Q. What bank? Where was the bank, was it in this country—in America?

A. *(mumbles)*

After the assassination of Abraham Lincoln, a Montreal bank advertised for heirs to claim a sizable bank account held in the name of John Wilkes Booth who had visited Canada six months before his crime. Edwin Booth would not allow any member of the family to claim the money.

Q. You have told me that Dr. Carter arrived in Washington a few days before the assassination. Where did he stay?
A. He stayed at the house . . . where I met him . . .
Q. Was it a house or a building?
A. . . . a house . . . owned by a member of the Circle.
Q. Was he using another name in Washington?
A. Who?
Q. Dr. Carter.
A. I don't understand. . . .
Q. Well, what I . . .
A. *(impatiently)* No one knew he was there . . . no one knew who he was . . . he was *unknown* because he was not associated with the North . . . or Washington . . . he was working for the Confederate Army. [At the time, this answer seemed contradictory because Booth had told me during previous questioning that Dr. Carter was from the Washington area.]

There were several things that bothered me. Booth had mentioned Dr. Carter almost from the beginning and continued to insist that he had been taken to him after being shot outside Ford's Theatre. I wrote to the American Medical Association in Washington and they could find no "Dr. Carter" in their records.

Booth's evasiveness continued to frustrate me, and during the next regression I did not try to conceal my irritation.

Q. You know very well where Dr. Carter was from and you will tell me!
A. *(quickly)* Baltimore.

Baltimore, Maryland, is less than an hour's drive from Washington and, strictly speaking, "in the Washington area." Perhaps at last I had a lead to Dr. Carter's identity. I wrote to the Enoch Pratt Free Library in Baltimore and they kindly sent a photostat of material regarding Charles Shirley Carter, found in the National Encyclopedia, Vol. 21, page 267.

It is stated that a Charles Shirley Carter was born April 2, 1840, in Clark County, Virginia. (This would make him two years younger than Booth.) Carter entered the University of Pennsylvania, Medical College, in 1860. (Booth told me he had met Carter in 1863 and that the latter was in college at the time.) Carter volunteered his services to the Confederate Army and served as an assistant surgeon until 1864, later as surgeon. He was stationed at Richmond when the war ended. (This corresponds to Booth's story that Carter had come to Washington from Richmond at the time of the assassination.)

At one time when I questioned Booth, he said that he and Carter had many interests in common. It is a matter of record that Booth loved horses and was a fine rider. In the biographical sketch of Dr. Carter it is noted that he was a great horseman who raised blooded animals.

After the Civil War, Dr. Carter practiced medicine in Baltimore. In 1867 he married the daughter of Thomas Swann, Governor of Maryland, and in 1868, the final year of the Governor's term, became his personal secretary. Swann then served four consecutive terms in Congress, and Carter remained at his side as his assistant. Swann died in 1883. I did not share the Carter information with Wesley, because I wanted to put more questions to Booth.

Q. Did you ever hear what happened to Dr. Carter after the war?

A. He went into a different field . . . but I don't know

what it was. He was usually taking care of people . . . but he left the medical profession after the war. He thought if he remained in practice—unless in the South—he would be scorned and ridiculed . . . and also might face charges of some sort . . . for being an officer in the Confederate Army. He thought that he would be better off in other work . . . where he would not receive ridicule . . . or whatever it was that . . . he was afraid of.

Q. If you had not been paid twenty-five thousand dollars to kill President Lincoln, do you think you would have done it anyway?

A. *(sadly or distantly)* I don't know . . . but I doubt very much that I would have.

17
THE SAN FRANCISCO EPISODE

Booth's escape to San Francisco from the Garrett Farm remained a mystery. He seemed to remember only that he boarded a stagecoach some distance from the farm and, traveling under the name of "James Benton," arrived at last in San Francisco after a long and rough journey.

When I could learn nothing more, I went on to question him about his reasons for being in San Francisco.

Q. Now, you have told me that after the assassination you went to San Francisco and used the name of "James Benton." Where did you live—do you know where you lived?
A. . . . S . . . s . . . seven.
Q. Seven something?
A. No . . .
Q. Do you know the name of the street?
A. *(coughs)*

Q. You can't remember the name of the street? Was it downtown—right downtown?

A. No . . . don't know *(mumbles)*.

Q. Don't let it bother you—you're tired. Do you know what month you left San Francisco on a ship, to go to England?

A. August or September. [In all other regressions he insisted that it was late in the year.]

Q. All right, John, can you tell me about the work you did for the Circle while you were in San Francisco, before you left the country?

A. After the assassination, Davy and I were to travel to San Francisco . . . Davy would have done almost anything I asked . . . he knew many things about Circle activities, and was quite adept at . . . doing his job. When Davy did not arrive in San Francisco to meet me, I knew that he had been captured . . . and I took it upon myself . . . to initiate the work . . . that he had been going to do. . . . There was much trouble in the area at that time . . .

Q. What kind of trouble?

A. . . . Trouble with the warehouses . . . the shipping warehouses . . . people trying to gain control. . . . They would burn a warehouse . . . or attack a ship . . . or people unloading a ship.

Q. Was San Francisco a major port?

A. No . . . not a major port . . . not like the eastern cities . . . but the Circle knew that one day . . . it would be a major port . . . and decided something would have to be done . . . to get rid of corruption.

Q. What did you do?

A. Well . . . I started a chain of events . . . not by myself . . . in other words, I did not go in person to people and talk to them . . . I used agents. . . . It took a certain amount of daring.

Q. Weren't you a little uneasy about being in San Francisco for such a length of time?

A. I was . . . toward the end . . . it was drawing out far longer than I wished to stay . . . but there wasn't anything I could do . . . the work had to be finished.

Q. John, did you think that the majority of the people would think you a hero because you had killed Lincoln?

A. No! That was the reason behind planning such an elaborate escape . . . the majority would not consider me a hero for killing the President.

Q. It has been said of you that you thought the South would make you a hero for having killed President Lincoln.

A. *(sharply)* They said that? . . . but that wasn't true at all! . . . There *was* no South . . . the South—that is the Confederacy—had died or was dying . . . killing President Lincoln wasn't done for anyone to become a hero . . . I knew this! . . . Perhaps some members of the Circle might have considered the assassination . . . an heroic act, but it was a matter of necessity! What really distressed me . . . the majority of the people did not realize what was going on . . . what Lincoln was doing . . . what his plans were . . . or what he had done. The majority—in the North and the South—did not know what kind of . . . person he was.

121

18
THE PRESIDENT AND SECRETARY OF WAR STANTON

THE NAME OF ABRAHAM LINCOLN HAS GONE DOWN IN HIS-
tory as one of our truly great Americans, and I suppose
that every one of us has a special feeling for the homely
man of the backwoods who made his way to the highest
office in the land—that of President of the United States.

When a man falls to the bullet of an assassin, he is
awarded a hero's crown. His past deeds are glorified and
death frees him from committing further errors, so that
he stands forever a monument of goodness and right. It
was disappointing to discover that when Booth discussed
Lincoln, there was a flaw in the pedestal.

Q. Would you say that President Lincoln was somewhat
weak in the manner of letting others make up his
mind for him?

A. Yes . . . I would say that was partly true . . . but
he was strong-headed in another way. . . . If he had
been so weak . . . as to allow others to make deci-

sions . . . it would have been easy . . . but this was not the case. . . . He wanted the country to react the way a small town reacts . . . to its major citizen . . . doing what he wished . . .

Q. I have heard that many people did not like Secretary of War Stanton, and that Lincoln seemed a little afraid of him.

A. Well . . . that was true . . . to an extent. . . . You see . . . Stanton was a member of the Circle . . . and he thought that the best way . . . to get Lincoln to do what he wanted . . . was to instill fear in him . . . and it almost amounted to telling him . . . that unless he did "such and such" . . . he would be killed.

Well . . . that was Stanton's way . . . that is the way Stanton thought it ought to be done . . . but Lincoln didn't go along. Apparently he . . . feared Stanton for a while . . . but then . . . he began to disbelieve him . . . but the thing he didn't realize . . . was that Stanton was telling him . . . - the truth. I didn't agree with that tactic . . . not the specific one that Stanton used . . . the threatening him . . . I didn't agree to that.

Q. But wasn't that better than killing him, if it could have been done that way?

A. Yes . . . but you see . . . there is a difference between someone . . . threatening your life . . . and someone *openly* threatening a man's life . . . so that he could turn around . . . accusingly . . . and say, "You threatened my life!" And in the case of a president . . . it's a little bit different.

Q. John, did Stanton have information about Lincoln that perhaps caused Lincoln to fear him?

A. I . . . don't understand.

Q. I mean, what made Lincoln allow Stanton to deliver such a threat?

A. Stanton wanted to get rid of Lincoln.

Q. Why instead, didn't Lincoln get rid of Stanton?

A. There were . . . several reasons.

Q. Can you tell me what they were?

A. *(shaking his head)*

Q. You can't tell me?

A. I can't seem to find . . . what was the question that you just asked me?

Q. I was asking why Lincoln put up with so much from Stanton?

A. When Mr. Lincoln was in Congress . . . he met Stanton . . . and they became good friends. Stanton was of no consequence politically . . . Lincoln was not of much consequence either, but he had the favor of a great many people . . . and the possibility of rising . . . to a high position . . . which he did.

    Lincoln was a man from a small town . . . a familiar saying was . . . "from the woods." He grew up a very poor man . . . and when he became President of the United States . . . this was not only bewildering to others . . . it was bewildering to him . . . he was not accustomed to the fine trappings of the White House.

    Stanton was an opportunist . . . and one who would do almost anything to gain power . . . to gain wealth . . . he was a very brilliant man . . . and . . . when Lincoln was elected President . . . he appointed Stanton to his cabinet. . . . I was unaware . . . at that time . . . of Stanton's greed.

Q. You never could tell about those people, could you, John.

A. Some things . . . were not publicized . . . the President was married . . . had children . . . and his marriage was having difficulties . . . Stanton was aware of this. . . . Shortly before the assassination . . . there was . . . well . . . there wasn't, but almost was . . . a scandal that would have

proved ruinous . . . to the President . . . and also . . . to the government.

Q. What was the scandal, John?

A. It involved a friend of Mr. Lincoln's . . . a woman.

Q. What was her name?

A. Rebecca . . . I can't think of her last name.

Q. Do you recall where she was from?

A. Don't know that I ever knew . . . other than
that . . . she was in Washington . . . at the
time . . . I wasn't interested . . . of use to Stanton, not to me . . . except indirectly.

Q. Did the situation become known?

A. The woman threatened to tell . . . I think she was
paid . . . if you wish to say that . . . or at least tak-
en care of . . . Stanton would use anyone . . . to
gain . . . what he wanted.

Q. John, you have told me that Lincoln and Stanton
were friends. It seems strange to me that he wanted
Lincoln killed.

A. Stanton was *not* the President . . . no matter how
much he wanted to be . . . no matter how much he
told the President what to do.

Q. Do you believe that it would have been a great disas-
ter had Stanton ever become president?

A. I didn't at the time . . . but later . . . as I became
better acquainted with Mr. Stanton . . . I knew
that it would have been . . . one of the worst
things . . . that could have happened.

Q. I have been wondering about something, John: If
Lincoln was uneducated, who do you suppose wrote
the "Gettysburg Address?"

A. Lincoln had one great gift . . . and that was probably why he decided to go into law. The only ability
he had at all . . . was the ability to talk . . . he
could put words together.

Q. What kind of a voice did he have, John?

A. It is hard to describe . . . it was higher than mine

126

. . . but not so high as to be upsetting. . . . It was unpleasant . . . however . . . if one listened to him for long periods of time . . . more than thirty minutes. . . . Because he could . . . speak well . . . he created an image that was advantageous. Of course . . . if people saw him before they had the opportunity to hear him speak . . . they would more than likely . . . leave.

Now Abraham Lincoln was dead. By shooting him, John Wilkes Booth had translated the President's eloquent words into sudden and violent action.

"The dogmas of the quiet past are inadequate to the stormy present . . . as our case is new, so must we think anew and act anew."

What was to become of the young actor who fled with every man's hand against him?

19
BOOTH ESCAPES TO ENGLAND

IN THE COURSE OF SEVERAL REGRESSIONS I TRIED TO GET Booth to talk about his escape from America to England, but he would not discuss the voyage and I could learn nothing more than that he had sailed on a vessel with the name Margaret in it, whose master's name was Henrichsen, sometime in the latter part of 1865.

Q. When you sailed from San Francisco for England, was it still 1865?
A. Yes, late in the year.
Q. When you landed in England, did you have identification papers?
A. Yes.
Q. Were they in the name of James Benton?
A. Yes . . . and there was another set of papers . . . in the name of William Sullivan.
Q. You had two sets of papers?

129

A. Yes . . . James Benton left the ship . . . went to a hotel . . . and registered. . . . In his room . . . he shaved his beard . . . trimmed his mustache . . . changed his clothes . . . and destroyed his identification papers . . . (*smiling*) He moved to an adjoining room . . . and became William Sullivan (*seems proud of quick-change act*).

Q. You destroyed the "Benton" papers—what about the baggage?

A. Actually . . . I didn't destroy the papers . . . didn't burn them. . . . I put them in my case . . . under the bottom . . . and left the "Benton" baggage in the "Benton" room. . . . It was taken over by another . . . member of the Circle.

Q. What happened to James Benton?

A. It had been established that he was . . . very old, and not well. . . . James Benton entered the country . . . and in a matter of two weeks . . . was dead. His papers were found on him . . . no questions asked.

Q. Were both sets of papers fixed in America?

A. It was not difficult.

Q. Were the papers fixed for you after the assassination, or before?

A. . . . A long time before . . . all of this had been very carefully arranged . . . my arrival date into England . . . the only uncertainty.

Q. Did William Sullivan have any relatives?

A. No . . . only his parents . . . and they had been dead for some time . . . no brothers . . . no sisters. . . . He was unmarried . . . and it proved convenient . . . the name had a certain twist to it that I liked.

Q. What was that?

A. Well . . . it was English . . . and yet in a way it was Irish . . . I could be either . . . as I chose.

Q. Were you about the same age as William Sullivan?

A. I was younger . . . but I looked the same age. . . . It wasn't difficult . . . I *was* older . . . but I doubted very much that . . . I would be recognized.

Q. Did you ever fully recover from your leg injury?

A. No . . . not entirely. . . . I continued to have a slight limp . . . I was aware of sharp pains at times . . . though I am not certain why the pain lingered on . . . I simply know that it did.

Q. When you entered France, you had to show papers also, didn't you?

A. Not at Calais.

Q. You didn't?

A. No . . . when I was going into Calais . . . I was going to see my relatives.

Q. Now, if you were coming into France to go to Paris or Calais or wherever, you would have had to show something, wouldn't you?

A. When I went from England to Calais . . . I didn't use any papers.

A. All right.

A. I had two sets of identification on me . . . but no government papers. . . . I went from England to Calais and back! When I came into England they thought that I was a British subject . . . and I didn't need papers. . . . When I went into Calais . . . they thought I was a citizen of Calais . . . and I didn't need any papers.

Q. All right, you have just told me that you had two sets of papers; one was Sullivan, what was the other?

A. Booth! *(angry and impatient)*

Q. I am trying to understand.

A. It was not a *government* document . . . but a piece of material . . . as identification. . . . Now it was different when I came from America to England . . . then I *had* to have a government document to enter the country.

131

Q. Yes, and those papers were in the name of "James Benton," and they turned up on some poor man who died. Was it a natural death?

A. *(remotely)* I wasn't concerned.

Q. You just didn't care about that?

A. I am not certain whether it was by natural means . . . or otherwise . . . I don't comprehend your difficulty in understanding—it's so simple!

Q. Yes, it is to you.

A. Well . . . *think!*

Q. I am thinking.

A. Now . . . when I went to England and to France . . . and to the other places I visited . . . I needed to have a government document to prove my identity. . . . Once I was in France there was no further checking . . . it was not at all uncommon for the English to travel to France . . . to Paris. . . . When I arrived in Paris . . . I could be whoever I wanted to be. . . . *Now* do you understand?

Q. Yes, John, I understand.

A. This particular set of papers which I used to get into France . . . or into other countries . . . had been prepared for me by the people who worked in the government in England . . . and were members of the Circle.

Q. You knew the right people, didn't you, John?

A. I don't know whether . . . right or wrong . . . they were just . . . doing their job.

As soon as I learned that Booth had escaped to England following the assassination, I questioned him about the location of the cottage where he stayed. Booth's memory was always vague for detail, but the initial difficulty was a misunderstanding on my part. I had understood him to say, "Londonderry," when I asked where the cottage was, and that is why our search was begun in that area.

132

Much later, and after a period of frustration, I found out that he had said, "London area."

Q. Let's talk about your property in England.
A. . . . Purchased by someone . . . acting for me . . . as me . . . so that when I arrived . . . name would be established . . . cause less suspicion.

I was five months late . . . in arriving . . . and someone was doubling for me . . . in house. . . . Took some strategy . . . whoever was in charge had done well. . . . People seemed aware . . . I had been ill . . . had my physician with me. . . . They were anxious to meet me . . . I came out of seclusion . . . met people.
Q. Was there any reason that you chose that part of England?
A. The Circle had purchased the property . . . it was secluded . . . yet close to London.

I had been working with Booth for almost a year and a half when I realized that I would need the help of a qualified researcher—one who was familiar with the Civil War period. I wrote to Arthur Sheehan in New York, and have been most grateful for his generous assistance and encouragement. Provided with the few clues that Booth had given me, Mr. Sheehan began at once the work of pinpointing the location of the cottage. He thought it was in the Gloucester area, but when I questioned Booth, he said that the village was some distance south of Gloucester.

In the next regression I posed as a stranger, hoping to trick Booth into being more precise. It turned out to be an amusing, but uninformative exchange:

Q. Why are you so quiet?
A. I am just admiring your beauty *(voice low and seduc-*

Q. *tive—long pause)* . . . You know . . . you are quite beautiful.

Q. Are you going to tell me the name of the village?

A. Why do you change to such a droll subject? . . . It was so pleasant . . . and you have to ask that. . . . What difference does it make?

Q. I would like to know what it is.

A. *(tauntingly)* If you must know . . . it is Glockenshire! [Booth accented the first and last syllables of the word, pronouncing *shire* with a long, drawled *i*.]

Q. Glockenshire? [I pronounced it just as he had.] I have heard of a place called Gloucester.

A. *(without expression)* Gloucester? . . . Yes, that is further north. [Was he disappointed that I had not guessed the name of the village? I could not tell from the tone of his voice, but one thing was certain—he was not going to tell me more, so I terminated the regression.]

The name of the village remained a mystery, and finding the cottage became of primary importance. It was there, Booth revealed, that he had taken positive steps to protect himself against possible death from the hands of Stanton and others who were in positions of power in America. I don't believe that Booth ever considered himself in real danger, but he was a cautious man.

Booth's anger grew, as time passed. He resented the fact that he alone bore the brunt of the assassination and was exiled, while other Circle members who had been part of the conspiracy climbed to greater power. Booth has said that Stanton and Seward began to pull away from the purposes of the Circle, and it was their involvement and their knowledge of the assassination that kept the Circle from punishing them. Booth brooded over the way that he had been used by Stanton and Seward; these men had plotted his death, and he had outwitted them. He had successfully escaped the country, but was he safe?

This question gnawed at Booth. He decided that if his enemies should contrive to kill him, America would know why. In the privacy of his English cottage, Booth wrote the entire account of the assassination, describing how it began, and listing the names of those involved. He mentioned certain "truths" that were in his keeping, and when he had finished the confession he put the papers in a box and buried it beneath a loose stone in the floor.

We never found Booth's cottage, nor the papers he claimed to have buried under the cottage floor. Booth mentioned this often, and during one of the regressions, I "suggested" that he try to reconstruct in writing some of his exposé. The following was written under hypnotic regression, May 22, 1971:

> *Only in case of my violent death would this be of any use to anyone. I, William Sullivan, am really John Wilkes Booth, the man who assassinated President Abraham Lincoln. My death being violent in nature, should reflect that someone in America thought I should be removed because I posed a threat to their existence, however, they knew this was untrue. Therefore it is noteworthy to explain who was involved in the plot to assassinate the president. There was an organization known as The Knights of the Golden Circle, which still exists today. This organization was responsible for the assassination and later change in government in not only the United States but also in most of Europe. Among the members were Secretary Stanton, Secretary Seward, President Andrew Johnson, F. J. Bush, John H. Adams and more to be revealed later in this exposé on the circle and its members. If they felt they could escape punishment they were wrong. It need only be looked into records to check that what I am saying is completely true.*

Booth often spoke of a trusted aide, Phillip Jourdain, a Circle member whom he had known for several years; they had become acquainted before the assassination.

Jourdain was the only member of Booth's staff in England who knew William Sullivan's true identity. Booth gave a sealed envelope to Phillip Jourdain and told him that if he were to die under mysterious circumstances, Jourdain was to open the envelope. If Booth died from natural causes, which he did, the envelope was to be burned without opening. The envelope contained directions for locating the papers, and the name of the addressee. Booth said that the man was trustworthy and would have followed his instructions to the letter.

Other members of Booth's staff knew that he traveled to different countries, but they did not know of his connections in Calais, nor of his use of the name "James Booth," while there. Post-mortem plans had been discussed, should Booth die some place other than in England. He said that there were two plans: one, that there would be a mock funeral in the English community where he had lived; two, if he died under an assumed name in another area, someone would come to the cottage to tell the townspeople that William Sullivan had moved, and to gather his belongings. Booth does not know which plan was put into effect at his death. He said that this had been left to the discretion of those in charge when it happened.

I questioned Booth further on the cottage location, about which my researcher, Arthur Sheehan, had provided background information:

Q. Did the property have a large amount of land with it?
A. A small amount . . . nothing in surrounding area . . . other than common land . . . small stream . . . trees . . . forest.
Q. How large was your cottage, John?
A. It was just a cottage.
Q. Did it have more than one room?
A. It had three areas.
Q. How old was the cottage, have you any idea?

136

A. Well . . . I would imagine that it was well over a hundred years old.

Q. Was it in good repair?

A. Oh, yes . . . well . . . not when I went there. . . . Many things needed to be done . . . and this occupied my spare time. . . . I had not been working regularly . . . in the theatre . . . and became very . . . very . . . bored.

Q. Did you purchase additional property?

A. I purchased a small piece of property . . . in Calais.

Q. Was there a river close to your property in England?

A. There was . . . not close . . . I don't know the distance. It took me about a quarter of a day . . . to get there.

Q. Does Amberley Castle mean anything to you?

A. It's north . . . north of the cottage.

Q. Was it also known as Amberley Common or Commons?

A. That was the area surrounding it. . . . It was sometimes called that . . . to designate the particular location . . . of the cottage . . . and other dwellings in . . . that area.

Q. How far away was the castle from your cottage?

A. If I looked north . . . I could see through the trees . . . the topmost part . . . of the castle.

Q. Was there a place near there called "The Devil's Churchyard?"

A. I had never been there . . . but did hear of such a place . . . it held no fascination for me, and I saw no reason to go there. . . . It was supposedly haunted . . . spirited . . . and that was the reason . . . for the name.

Q. Evil spirits?

A. I presume so . . . perhaps just spirits . . . one never knew whether they were . . . evil or good.

20
BOOTH RETURNS TO THE FOOTLIGHTS

BOOTH HAD RETURNED TO ENGLISH SOIL AND THE HOME of his forefathers. William J. Sullivan was free from any link to America: John Wilkes Booth was truly dead.

Somewhere deep in the veins of Booth ran the theatrical blood of his father, the great Shakespearean actor, Junius Brutus Booth, and John was to discover that merely by changing his name, he could not suppress an aching need to return to the stage. Just as a moth is inevitably drawn to the flame, so Booth was recalled to the London theatres.

Q. During the years you worked in the Circle, was there any time your name appeared in the papers?
A. Which name?
Q. The name you were using then.
A. Not to my knowledge.
Q. Now, in England you were using the name of Sullivan?

A. Yes . . . I'm . . . there was an incident when my name appeared . . . in a review of a production . . . at a theatre in London. . . . I only had a small part . . . only four lines . . . I was on stage perhaps twenty minutes. For some reason, the reviewer singled me out . . . why . . . I wasn't quite sure . . . as being the most believable person with a small part in the show. . . . Would all other actors work as hard as I . . . perhaps production would be better. . . . I was embarrassed that my name appeared in print.

Q. When was this?

A. The production was in December of 1870 . . . I believe.

Q. Do you recall the name of the theatre?

A. I'm not certain . . . I believe it had "Royal" in it.

Q. Well, there probably weren't more than one or two theatres in London at that time?

A. There were at least three or four . . . commendable London theatres.

As soon as I had the information that Booth had returned to the London stage, I asked for a search of the records in the theater collection of the Library and Museum of the Performing Arts at Lincoln Center in New York. The theatrical magazine in London during those years was *The Era;* in it was mentioned an actor, J. O'Sullivan, who had a small part in an Irish play in 1869. Arthur Sheehan sent me copies of the lists that included the name, and it did not appear beyond the time that Booth had lived.

When I asked Booth if he had changed his name for stage purposes, he smiled and answered, "I merely added a bit o' the Irish to it." Wesley was not told this, although I had long ago discarded the suggestion that he could influence Booth in any way. I always protected any research material carefully.

While reading through the lists of actors' names that my researcher had sent me from New York, I came across the name of "Boothroyd Fairclough," who had played Shakespearian roles during the same years as Booth. I wondered if this might mean something, so I questioned him about it.

Q. Who was Boothroyd Fairclough?
A. It was a name that I used upon occasion.
Q. On the stage?
A. Yes.
Q. Where did the name come from?
A. I made it up.

I had the strange feeling that the name was not made up. I can't explain this, but I learned that Fairclough had been acting years before in New York, during the career of John Wilkes Booth. This proved to be a most valuable clue. Boothroyd Fairclough appeared in "Hamlet" at the London Lyceum Theatre in September, 1868. The theatre manager, E. T. Smith, said he had engaged the actor because of favorable reviews he had received for performances in the United States. The American Boothroyd Fairclough's few appearances can be found in Odell's history of the New York stage. They show an actor who was anything but a star and would have seemed a poor choice for the Danish prince, Hamlet. On October 4, 1868, Fairclough's performance as Othello at the Lyceum Theatre drew enthusiastic comment in the London *Times*. Other reviews of his 1868 appearances were also discussed in this journal, and can be found in The New York Public Library newspaper library. I challenged Booth again about the actor's name.

Q. You didn't make it up.
A. *(smiling)* He didn't have the complete name
Q. Oh yes he did, John, the man's name was Boothroyd

Fairclough. Now how did you know that you would be safe using his name?

A. *(puzzled)* The man was no longer around! [I could almost see his mind working, wondering how I knew all of this.]

Q. What happened to him?

A. He just . . . disappeared.

Q. Disappeared?

A. One day he moved . . . and he never showed up anywhere else.

Q. Did you resemble the man?

A. Not really . . . he was taller than I . . . and had broader shoulders.

Q. Dark complexion?

A. More so than I.

Q. Do you remember where you met him?

A. Through the Circle.

Q. Was he a member?

A. No . . . not a member . . . he worked for the Circle . . . not part of the planning . . . only told what to do. He did not agree to the assassination of the President . . . wanted to get away.

Booth said that because Fairclough had been associated with the Circle for some time, had been a good worker, it was decided to transfer him somewhere where he would not be in jeopardy. He boarded a ship and sailed to England under an assumed name, but was met by Booth's men who questioned him and decided that he would be a threat to the Circle, wherever he was. "He was . . . therefore," according to Booth, "removed from the roster."

Q. He wasn't much of an actor, was he?

A. On the contrary . . . he was relatively decent . . . but he was better paid for his work outside the theatre."

Some of the members of the Circle were aware of my past . . . and of my activities in the theatre . . . and were not pleased. When I would use an assumed name . . . this particular name . . . they were certain that someone would discover who I was.

Q. I suppose that's true. Where did the man get such a strange name though? I don't believe that I have ever heard of a name like Boothroyd!

A. With the name of "Booth" and the family of "Boyd" . . . and the "fair cloud" in the sky.

Booth seemed to possess a somewhat bizarre sense of humor and it was quite apparent that he enjoyed his little joke on the audience. Unlike a comedian who shares himself with the audience, Booth played for himself. He was the onlooker as well as the performer. His silent laughter rang only in his own ears and he was satisfied.

21
THE STRANGE BOOTH FAMILY

Q. Did it never bother you to know that your sister was living in London?

A. Perhaps you might call it excessive egotism on my part . . . but I was convinced that had my sister seen me . . . she would not have known who I was.

Q. You had changed so much?

A. Not necessarily . . . she was simply not observant.

Q. Surely, if she had seen you, she would have recognized you.

A. She had all the information concerning the body that was found . . . and she knew it could not possibly have been me . . . She had not seen the body . . . but she knew enough to be certain . . . that I was alive.

Asia *wanted* me dead . . . If she had run into me by accident . . . she would have considered it a coincidence . . . to have seen someone who *looked* like her "late brother." I had nothing to worry about . . . she had wished me dead for a year before I . . . supposedly . . . died.

Q. But your mother and Edwin knew, for a fact, that you were living.

A. They had no reason to say anything . . . they had already buried me.

Q. It is difficult for me to understand why they felt that way.

A. Mother was old . . . and her mind played tricks on her. . . . She knew that I was alive . . . but had no way of proving it. . . . So far as Edwin was concerned . . . he thought . . . and he was right . . . that I was better off if the government considered me dead. . . . He knew that if he ever said anything . . . he would find *himself* dead.

Q. Someone would have killed him?

A. I am not necessarily saying that someone would have killed him. . . . I am only saying that he would have found himself dead. . . . Edwin was greedy . . . always had been. . . . He liked money and the alcohol it could buy for him. . . . Finding me alive would have very much cramped his alcoholic intake . . . and that he couldn't stand.

Q. But he knew that you were alive.

A. Only privately . . . not publicly.

Q. You came from a strange family, didn't you, John?

A. Not at all! . . . It was simply that we knew how to buy people off. . . . Edwin had a problem . . . alcohol . . . he liked alcohol . . . and he needed the money to buy it. . . . By making certain that he had the money . . . through his endeavors at acting . . . supposedly . . . it was quite easy to keep him in enough alcohol. . . . He was . . . in fact . . . quite well preserved. There were many times when people would no longer hire him . . . or had thought about not hiring him . . . when I would talk to people I knew . . . and they would pull strings . . . to make certain that Edwin was employed . . . and making enough money. Actually . . . the same thing goes for my mother . . . her money ran out eventually . . . or at least a large part of it . . . but she was allowed to stay in the house . . . and there was always plenty of food on the table. . . . This too . . . was taken care of.

Q. Tell me about your other brother . . . Junius Brutus Booth.

A. There really is not much to tell . . . I did not know him well. . . . He was older . . . and in the family tradition . . . he did some acting . . . but I really know very little about him.

Q. What about Rosalie?

A. We played together . . . upon occasion. . . . She stayed in the house most of the time. . . . Eventually she married . . . and stayed with her husband. . . . It was almost as if she were no longer a part of the family. [Rosalie never married.]

22
A SPOTLIGHT ON THE CIRCLE

BECAUSE THE POWER AND INFLUENCE OF THE KNIGHTS OF the GOLDEN CIRCLE appeared to be widespread, I have tried to limit Booth's exposé to members who, in one way or other, were associated with the assassination of President Lincoln.

Q. If the Circle was a secret organization, why did you leave evidence of your affiliation to be found after the assassination?

A. Again . . . please?

Q. After the assassination, there was some material found in your trunk; it showed an affiliation with the Circle, and I am wondering why you left it?

A. If I recall correctly . . . the information . . . left behind . . . and possibly found by someone . . . only partly linked me . . . to the Circle. . . . It did not implicate them with the assassination *(jaw muscles tighten; words are brittle; shows suppressed anger*

149

as continues): It was left as a warning to Stanton! . . . Stanton was aware . . . or I had attempted to make him aware . . . that I had prepared a thoroughly detailed and documented history of the . . . activities of the Circle . . . which would implicate *him*

Q. What was it you left?

A. If I recall correctly . . . it seems that I left . . . a letter. . . . perhaps two letters . . . a receipt . . . a bill. . . . I wasn't interested in what was found . . . only that Stanton was . . . aware of the find. . . . I'm sure that he paid dearly to have it . . . hushed up . . .

Q. Lafayette Baker was the man who headed the search for the "supposed" Booth who died at the Garrett farm. Did you know this man? [Lafayette C. Baker, Chief of the United States Detective Bureau, has been referred to as the "father of the Secret Service." He received $15,000 of the reward offered by the War Department, as having supplied the brains for Booth's capture. It has been suggested (*Civil War Times*, Aug. 1961) that after Baker's death a coded message was found in which he accused Stanton of plotting the murder of Abraham Lincoln.]

A. Not personally . . . no.

Q. He must have worked for the Circle, didn't he?

A. He worked for Stanton!

Q. John, after Lincoln was assassinated, did you ever think, or was it ever mentioned, that he might not be the last president to be assassinated in this country?

A. You mean in America?

Q. Yes.

A. I imagine that if . . . at a later time . . . or in later years . . . the need arose . . . to bring about a particular goal . . . an assassination would be . . . undertaken again. . . . It was always considered a . . . last resort.

Q. Were the goals that the Circle set for itself accomplished?

A. *(A look of surprise crosses "Booth's" face)* Certainly not! Many of the goals were set far beyond my lifetime, perhaps a hundred years in advance.

Q. John, you remember the "Mr. Richards" who waited for you in the carriage after the assassination—what happened to him?

A. He continued to work with the Circle . . . in a limited way. . . . The Circle did not want someone who might . . . suspect anything . . . some members of the government who were not Circle members . . . were interested in doing a study of the assassination . . . trying to find out what happened. . . . of course . . . it was of the utmost importance . . . that those directly connected . . . be heard from as little as possible . . . not put into a position where they might . . . draw public attention.

Q. After the assassination, Stanton blamed Jefferson Davis and the radicals, linking you with them. Why did he do that?

A. Actually . . . that was part of the plan. . . . It is obvious that the assassination . . . the attack on Seward's life . . . the planned attack on Stanton . . . and others . . . could not in any way . . . be linked to them. . . . There needed to be someone . . . on whom to place the blame . . . should there be any question of conspiracy.

   I understand that it became necessary . . . that Stanton made his accusations . . . realizing that Jefferson Davis . . . and his allies . . . had little to defend themselves with. . . . After the war . . . many . . . many people were against Davis and his allies . . . because of the trouble . . . the disruption . . . the war itself.

Q. Wasn't this coming very close to Mr. Benjamin?

151

[Judah P. Benjamin was Secretary of War, and later Secretary of State, under Jefferson Davis, President of the Confederacy.]

A. Oh, but the allies of the South . . . even Mr. Benjamin . . . "Mr. Ben" we called him . . . were not that necessary. . . . You see . . . Mr. Benjamin . . . who was a part of the southern government . . . although partially linked with the Circle . . . was not directly connected . . . the Circle simply worked through him . . . and used him. . . . There was another . . . "Mr. Benjamin" . . . who was in the North . . . at least that was the name he used . . .

Booth identified "Mr. Benjamin" from the North as Benjamin Laughton, New York banker and importer, and claimed that he was a very high-ranking member of the Circle who took care of financial matters in America, and managed Circle funds abroad. This "Mr. Benjamin" was described by Booth as having many elaborate disguises. Booth said that he often introduced himself as "Mr. Benjamin" when he was in Europe—"Benjamin," "Sullivan," "Wilkes," "De Voe,"—depending on the situation.

Q. All right, John, you have said that the "Mr. Benjamin" who was part of the Confederacy was not a member of the Circle. Was Jefferson Davis a member?

A. Jefferson Davis was not!

Q. He wasn't?

A. No! . . . No! . . . he was *not* a member of the Circle.

Q. Sometimes as I talk to you, John, I have the impression that you didn't fully agree with the Confederate government in the South. Perhaps you might make this clear for me.

A. What I didn't agree with was . . . they were going to

fight for their principles . . . and what they stood for. . . . They were going to work as a . . . separate country . . . but they failed to consider . . . what this might mean.

Many were fighting because they . . . didn't want their land taken away from them . . . but it got to the point . . . no one knew exactly . . . who was going to do the . . . taking.

They failed to have enough foresight to maintain . . . proper relations with foreign countries . . . so they could maintain with sufficient food . . . and supplies. . . . They failed to get support . . . from any other country. . . . It was all jumbled up.

Q. Were the goals of the Circle in other countries the same as the goals of the Circle in America?

A. The Circle always . . . maintained the same basic goals . . . ideals . . . and concepts.

Q. John, when you undertook the Circle work in Europe, you must have received a guarantee of a substantial amount of money. After all, you were an actor of some reputation, and had been making a great deal of money.

A. You mean . . . from Circle funds?

Q. Yes, certainly they were going to pay you for your services?

A. There were certain . . . monetary rewards from the Circle . . . but that was not my main source . . . of income.

Q. I see. Did you have little business deals on the side?

A. I was involved in several . . . private businesses . . .

Q. Do you remember any meetings where information was exchanged for money?

A. Not information . . . not from me . . . not for money.

Q. Not if it were connected with the Circle?

A. No.

Q. You didn't sell information?

A. Never! *(answers firmly)*

Q. That surprises me.

A. There were people who did . . . but they were duly taken care of.

Q. Did you ever have any apprehension that caused you to bury the confession of the assassination beneath your cottage floor?

A. No . . . I wouldn't say that it was apprehension . . . but perhaps . . . that would be the word. . . . It would appear to be fear . . . but it wasn't. . . . I knew Stanton . . . and I knew him well! . . . He had underestimated me several times. . . . I had not gauged him as well as I should have . . . but I never discounted his ability . . . especially when I found out what he had done after the assassination.

Q. How many people in Europe knew who you really were?

A. It was not necessary to know who I was!

Q. When you used the name of "Mr. Benjamin," were you actually posing as "Mr. Benjamin?"

A. Whatever name I used . . . I assumed that role . . . What do you mean by posing?

Q. I mean, did other people think you were the person whose name you were using?

A. I assumed an identity . . . usually "Mr. Benjamin" . . . and sometimes used make-up . . . or certain clothing . . . only for secrecy . . . or cover . . . should anyone check. . . . I must say . . . that was the most difficult acting . . . I had ever done.

Q. I should imagine so! Didn't you ever become frightened?

A. If fear had been a part of my make-up . . . I never would have succeeded!

154

Q. I suppose that is true, John, but it does seem rather frightening to me.

A. I think that there were only two times . . . in my life . . . when I was afraid.

Q. What were those times?

A. Just before . . . the assassination . . . and another time in . . . Calais.

Q. Tell me, John.

A. *(sits silently, his face very old and sad)*

Q. Was this just before your death?

A. *(hoarse whisper)* Yes.

23
CALAIS AND BOOTH'S FINAL DAYS

I HAVE OFTEN BEEN ASKED THE QUESTION, "WHY DOESN'T Booth speak openly about his life, if it is over? What can he fear?"

After killing President Lincoln, Booth suffered a traumatic shock. He never remembered the actual shooting, and when he left the United States, he tried to block out everything. Secrecy and caution, the safeguards that allowed him to remain free from detection, became a deeply interwoven thread in the pattern of his personality. During regressions, I often had to stop to reassure him that his old life was over, but in some instances he didn't accept my reassurance, nor seem to fully understand what I was saying.

Q. When I ask you questions, as I'm asking you now, do you hear the answers and then tell them to me?
A. What?
Q. When I ask you about your life, John, that you've

    lived and you realize is over, are you remembering that life, or are you hearing the answers and then giving them to me?

A. I just see flashes.

Q. You just see flashes?

A. Pictures . . . I don't understand the question.

Q. Were you aware that you were going to live again?

A. Yes.

Q. How did you know?

A. The life appeared as a pinpoint of light, a distant star. I was traveling toward it.

Q. Did you have a choice of lives?

A. It was my second chance and the only one available.

Recently, I noticed that Booth's right arm from the elbow down had risen from the chair and was trembling uncontrollably. I asked if he had trouble with his hand or arm, and he said that after the assassination, on the trip across the country, his hand began to tremble, and he had no control over it. I asked if he thought it related to the assassination, and he answered, "It seems strange that I had no trouble before that time."

"Were you frightened?" I asked.

"No . . ." he answered me, "I just thought that it would be all right in time."

"How long were you bothered with it?"

"It went away in about two years," he said.

Inside the diary that had belonged to Booth, and was found on the body of the man who died at the Garrett Farm, was an old picture postcard portraying a family—a mother and father and two children—sitting in the comfortable surroundings of a parlor. It bore no outward significance, and apparently had no meaning for anyone but Booth, but perhaps it was a symbol of his deep longing for family ties, a longing which took him back at last to Calais, France.

Questioning Booth about his life in Calais was sometimes difficult because, although his final years were the easiest for him to remember, he had hoped to find peace in this French seaport town, and was saddened when his thoughts returned there.

Gervais Booth, John told me, was the son of his father's brother and his own first cousin; he was a partner or part owner of a Calais lace factory in which John claimed to hold a substantial interest.

Q. What made you renew your family associations in Calais?

A. When I left America . . . I left all behind . . . family . . . everyone. . . . Although in England . . . I made many new acquaintances . . . many new friends . . . one becomes lonely for a family.

Q. When you left your cottage in England to go to Calais, how did you go?

A. By boat . . . only way to go . . . left Portsmouth in the evening . . . and on landing in France . . . I would get a carriage . . . to continue my journey.

Q. How far from Portsmouth was the village in which you lived?

A. From half to three quarters of a day's ride . . . depending on the weather.

Q. Just before your death had you gone to Calais with the intention of staying there?

A. Once every six months . . . sometimes more often . . . I would venture to Calais . . . to take care of interests there . . . and to be with my family. . . . At that time . . . I planned to extend my visit. . . . I never left . . .

159

Q. Had you been ill while you were in England or did the illness come on suddenly in France?

A. I had suffered periods of illness . . . over the previous years . . . but not a sign that . . . death . . . would be forthcoming.

Q. You must have had some money in a London bank; have you any idea what happened to it after your death?

A. No . . . some of it was under the . . . Sullivan name . . . I was able to withdraw · · · money from . . . other funds . . . but others could . . . also. . . . There was only one account under my name . . . in London . . . and only I had access to it.

Q. Do you remember the name of the bank?

A. The Bank of London.

Q. Did you make provisions for money in the London bank?

A. No . . . there was money in the bank in London . . . and bank in Calais. . . . Money in Calais was set aside . . . for my family.

Q. Your wife, or Booth family?

A. Wife (*low tone*).

Q. John, when did you go to Calais for the first time?

A. I believe it was 1860 . . . possibly . . . '59.

Q. How did you know of the relatives in Calais?

A. My father told me of them.

Q. Was Gervais the only person related to you in Calais?

A. No . . . Gervais had a sister.

Q. Now, when you went to Calais, what name did you use there?

A. James William Booth.

Q. Was this a name taken from someone else?

A. No.

Q. It was fictitious?

A. Yes.

Q. Did Gervais know that you had not been born in Calais?

A. He knew where I had been born . . . and he was aware of my family.

Q. He knew who you *really* were?

A. Yes.

Q. Was Gervais a member of the Circle?

A. No.

Q. Was he the only one in Calais who knew who you were?

A. . . . Only business partner . . . and a relative. He was aware of what I'd done in America . . . also knew reasons why I'd done this . . . probably one of the closest relatives and friends I ever had.

Q. All right, John, let's go back. When you went to Calais for the first time in 1859 or '60 did you go under your own name?

A. No . . . I did not!

Q. Why?

A. I didn't want anyone to know that . . . I had left the country.

Q. Why didn't you want anyone to know?

A. Because I wasn't supposed to be . . . out of the country. . . . At the time I was on holiday . . . I had been working very hard . . . and needed some rest. . . . My father had told me about England . . . and about the relatives . . . in France. . . . I decided to visit them.

Q. Now, was that the only trip you made there until just before the assassination?

A. Yes. [It is recorded in the journal of the French tragedian, Edmond Got, that Booth was a guest at his house in Paris, just three months before the assassination. *L'assassinat du président Lincoln,* wrote Got on April 30, 1865—*et je connais le principal acteur*—and I know the principal actor.]

Q. How were you sure that Gervais would not give you away when you went there after the assassination?

A. I was in touch with Gervais . . . from England . . . and an agreement was reached. . . . Gervais was true to the family name of Booth . . . he would not have betrayed me.

Q. Wasn't Gervais rather shocked to see you?

A. Well . . . not in Calais. . . . Actually, Gervais' worry was . . . that I would be found . . . therefore . . . he made the name change official . . . within the family.

Q. John, tell me about the woman you married in Calais.

A. She was really . . . no one in particular.

Q. What do you mean?

A. I mean . . . she had no social connections. . . . I loved her . . . she was the only woman I ever truly loved. . . . She was a great comfort to me . . . but she was not aware of what was going on . . . I'm certain of that. . . . She was nice . . . she was simple . . . she was considerate and she . . . I believe . . . loved me very much.

Q. John, when you speak of your wife in Calais, tell me why you call her "Mary" part of the time and again, you refer to her as "Marie?"

A. Her name was Marie . . . but I called her Mary. . . . some of the time it depended upon my mood . . .

Q. Wasn't her real name Henriette Eagle?

A. That name . . . how I detest that name! . . . 'Twas a man's name . . . not a name that belonged to my Mary . . . my Marie . . . so warm . . . so tender.

Q. But that was her real name? [I was quite certain of this because of Booth's references to her.]

A. Yes . . . although I never considered it so!

Q. What kind of work did her father do?

A. He always worked . . . I am not certain what he did . . . during the time that I knew him . . . he was always around the docks . . . working there.

Q. Did she have a brother?

A. There were other children in the family . . . I don't remember exactly . . . you see . . . before we were married . . . we just spent our time together . . . I wasn't interested in her . . . family . . . only in her.

Q. Was she a friend of Gervais' family?

A. Yes . . . that was how we met.

Q. What did her family think of the marriage?

A. So far as I know . . . they were against it . . . at the beginning anyway . . . although I am certain that they were happy to see her . . . married . . . she was past marriageable age . . . had not been married before.

Q. Were you married in church?

A. No.

Q. No?

A. At the time of the wedding . . . she was with child.

Q. John, when you were married and living in Calais as James Booth, did you attempt to change your signature?

A. A different name . . . made a difference.

Q. I know that, John, but did you attempt to alter your handwriting?

A. Yes . . . there were changes . . . some just occurred.

Q. When you went to Calais, and you signed your name, Booth, did you make changes?

A. Somewhat . . . yes . . . there really wasn't much change . . . I didn't sign it often. [I remembered when Wesley as "Booth" had signed his autograph —"To Suzanne, from J.W. Booth." John or James?]

Q. You would have been more careful if you had signed a permanent record, would you not?

A. I attempted to be . . . yes.

Q. John, I am going to ask you a question, and I am sure you know the answer. When you were on your death-bed, why didn't your wife come to you? [During early regression Booth had maintained that his wife had been at his bedside when he left the Booth life. Later, he painfully admitted that this was not true—she had not come to him.]

A. (*long pause*)

Q. John, I do not believe that Gervais really went to fetch Marie.

A. He came back . . . and he didn't want to . . . tell me . . . he began to cry. . . . he said she . . . wouldn't come . . . he said she had gone to a relative . . . I don't even know . . . to which one . . . I called for Mary many times.

Q. Have you *no* idea why she didn't come to you?

A. I'm not certain.

Q. When you say "not certain," I have the feeling that you *do* know.

A. About a week before I became ill . . . I told her that . . . I had to go away . . . on business to England . . . I didn't want to go!

Q. Did you quarrel?

A. We . . . had some words.

Q. I see.

A. . . . But whenever I returned to Calais . . . I would always go immediately . . . to her! Just about three nights before I died . . . I went to Gervais' house . . . there had been trouble at the factory . . . and I went over to talk to him. . . . It was raining that evening . . . a little cold . . . and I guess I didn't put on enough wrap.

I walked over . . . it wasn't very far. . . . I hadn't wanted to take time—to get the horse and saddle him—and when I left Gervais . . . I walked home. . . . Mary was already in bed.

164

When I awoke . . . the next day. . . . I knew I wasn't well . . . but I didn't know how serious it was. . . . I went to the factory . . . became worse. . . . Gervais' house was closer to the factory . . . than mine was . . . and he brought me there . . . to lie down . . . Jourdain came to see me and I never got up again. [The Jourdains were also prominent in the lace business in England.]

They called a nurse . . . not really a nurse . . . but a woman . . . who looked after the sick. . . . She tried several remedies . . . before the doctor came.

I wanted so much to see . . . my wife . . . wanted her to be at my side. . . . I was too ill to go home . . . I don't know why Mary didn't come. . . . When Gervais came back . . . and she wasn't with him . . . I knew that there was no use . . . waiting any longer. . . . I loved her . . . but I guess she . . . didn't love me.

Q. I don't believe that, John.
A. . . . The worst part . . . I thought that I had . . . gone to sleep . . . but suddenly . . . I was looking at myself asleep. . . . Everyone else in the room . . . was crying. . . . I couldn't understand it . . . I tried to reach them . . . talk to them . . . but they wouldn't hear me.
Q. Listen to me, John. Gervais and Jourdain *knew* . . . that you were John Wilkes Booth. Marie and the doctor and the nurse believed that you were James Booth. Could Gervais and Jourdain have run the risk of a deathbed confession to your wife?
A. I would not do that . . . what would I have gained?
Q. You were very ill with a high fever, John. You might have been delirious. Sometimes people talk when they are near death.
A. There would have been no reason. [I took Booth over the death scene several times, trying to make him see

165

the logic of what I believed to be the truth, but he continued to insist that Marie had deliberately deserted him in his last hours.]

Q. Your life was filled with such tragedy, John, were there ever times when you were happy?

A. Oh yes . . . but most of the time . . . it was only a false happiness . . . merely a show . . .

Q. Had you thought, before your death, that death was the end of everything?

A. It's difficult to remember . . . what one's thoughts were . . . one seldom thinks about death. . . . It is so final—at least everyone thinks it is final—it seems so . . . frightening.

I don't know that all deaths are like mine . . . where it feels as though one was going to sleep . . . I guess that is what I am doing now . . . looking at myself . . . asleep. . . . It's a strange feeling . . . I feel as though I had a body . . . I can see it . . . not as an image . . . I can *see* it . . . but it has no life.

Of course . . . one can't experience more than one death. . . . I don't know . . . what it would have been like had I been . . . shot and killed . . .

24
THE INCREDIBLE JOURNEY

As John Wilkes Booth's life after the assassination unfolded, I felt an urgent desire to go to England and France. I asked Wesley if he would accompany my husband, Lenny, and me, for surely Booth must be part of the venture.

Wesley was reluctant at first, and would not tell me why, but under hypnosis he admitted that he was afraid he would disappoint me in being unable to recall incidents in the Booth life. I tried to reassure him, begging him to relax. I wanted him to be completely honest about what he felt, or did not feel, but as the day of departure drew near, my own anxiety increased.

I knew that I was taking a subject back to retrace his footsteps in a former life, and that he had been subjected to many hours of in-depth hypnosis. As a precaution, I conditioned Wesley so that a light touch on the forehead would place him instantly into the hypnotic state. Should Booth begin to overwhelm him in the conscious state, I would have immediate control.

167

We left September 6, 1971, laden with cameras, a tape recorder, and notebooks—prepared for a two week stay. Neither Wesley nor I had been abroad, and my husband, although overseas during the last war, had not been to England or France. A rented car was waiting for us at the London airport, where we landed after an uneventful flight. The car, a small English model, did not have automatic shift. Lenny has a leg defect so could not drive; I do not drive, leaving Wesley—seated in an unfamiliar right hand driver's seat—to take the wheel as we barged into the early morning traffic.

The amazing result of Wesley's driving was that he *knew where he was going.* He pointed out landmarks to us as if we were tourists and London was "his town," and somehow managed to find our hotel without any difficulty.

In the afternoon we planned to sight-see, and took a bus downtown to "Picadilly Circus." We were walking in front of the old Lyric Theatre when Wesley stopped suddenly and went into the lobby, passing through and into the main part of the theatre where he studied the interior for a moment before going up to the man collecting tickets.

"When did they make the changes in this theatre?"he demanded. The man looked at him blankly; I had caught up with Wesley and led him outside. He was like a sleep walker, and continued around to the back of the theatre where he seemed puzzled not to be able to find the stage door. There appeared to be nothing there but a few shabby shops and a pub, but Wesley kept walking back and forth muttering that the stage door had been at the rear. Finally, he turned into a small alley.

"I see," he commented. "They have added this back part and changed the stage door."

At the Theatre Museum we were disappointed because records went back only to 1904, but at the British Museum where files of old newspapers are kept, we discovered that during the years when "Booth" claimed to have lived in England, every London newspaper published lists of "Actors Wanted"; the chief qualification—that an actor have money to buy his costumes—would have presented no hardship for Booth. I remembered that he had said, "Finding work as an actor in London was not at all difficult."

We left London the next morning for Gloucester, where we tried unsuccessfully to trace the property of William Sullivan; then drove to Painswick, in the Stroud district, less than ten miles from Amberley. I recalled that Booth had said he could see Amberley Castle—"the topmost part"—from his cottage. If luck were with us, we might find that cottage!

Painswick was a charming village with winding streets and old stone houses. We found rooms for the night in a small comfortable inn across from an old cemetery. After supper Wesley suggested a walk, but he turned away from us abruptly, to wander through the cemetery. He seemed a stranger to us, lost in his own thoughts, and in the dim light appeared to walk with a limp. Wesley was to repeat this behavior during the trip, and each time it left us with a feeling of uneasiness.

When we returned to the inn, Wesley complained of being drowsy, but we sat for a while in the pub—a friendly place where the innkeeper came to join us. He proved to be a willing conversationalist and in answer to our questions, told us that the district had been built on the wool industry; that its residents at one time had used wool to trade instead of money. Now I understood why Booth had not remembered Stroud, although I had questioned him about it; at present, it was a sizable community and the county seat, but in Booth's time it must have been just a hamlet with a few scattered cottages. We wondered if the cottage we looked for could have been among them?

The next morning we drove around the district and after a while found ourselves on a high ridge overlooking the Severn River valley. Wesley had grown increasingly quiet during the drive and now, without warning, pulled the car off the roadway and parked. He gave no explanation, but opened the door and stepped out into a biting wind. He was not wearing a coat but seemed oblivious to the cold as he walked the short distance to a lookout point. A soft blue haze hung loosely in the cradle of the valley where dozens of cottages dotted the sloping hillsides.

Wesley stood silently, his eyes fixed on the scene below. His face, etched with deep lines, looked older, and he was crying.

Lenny and I watched Wesley, and waited with our cameras in hand, but neither of us could take a picture of him. To have intruded upon his privacy at that moment would have seemed cruel. Wesley continued to stand this way for several minutes, and when at last I nudged him and called his name, he swung slowly around to look at me as Orpheus might have looked at Eurydice—one backward glance full of longing and despair. Then he turned suddenly, and walked to the car.

The next day Wesley was not his usual self, but quiet, moody, and difficult. He asked if he might rent a horse and ride through the coutryside in search of the cottage, but I rejected this proposal as far too risky. When I questioned Wesley about his feelings, he answered that they were difficult to put into words, but that the sight of the valley had filled him with a deep sadness, and a realization that he could never return to the peace he had known there.

We returned to London, and the following day boarded a ferry from Dover to Calais. Lenny was not feeling well, and I did what I could to make him comfortable in the cabin before following Wesley on deck; he had fallen abruptly silent and I trailed a short distance behind him.

As we neared Calais, Wesley stood with his hands gripping the railing. He seemed not to notice the sharp, chill wind as he peered through the fog at the ragged outline of the shore. Once again his face appeared old and drawn, and he was weeping without a sound.

Wesley told me that his first thought had been, "God, I'm coming home!" Then he realized that he was Wesley and tried to hold onto the reality of himself, but he could feel it slip as he was caught in the powerful grip of the Booth memory.

We had difficulty finding a place to stay after we landed, and spent an uneasy night. Lenny had become quite ill and I felt panicky in a strange land, with a sick husband and no one to help us, but in the morning Lenny was much improved, and our spirits rose. We rented a car and located the town historian who told us in halting English that there were two cemeteries in Calais. He said that the Booths of the lace factory were buried in one of them, but he didn't know which one. He had pronounced the name, "Boot."

We met with very little success at the first cemetery and returned to our hotel discouraged. Wesley thought that I should regress him, and when I did, he seemed to have no knowledge that his physical body was in Calais, and took the same length of time to answer my questions as he had during other regressions. I regressed him to his last days in Calais:

Q. John, can you tell me where your family buried your body when you left it in Calais?

A. A small private cemetery . . . north of town. [He had called it *Le Jardin de Plaisir*—the Garden of Pleasure.]

Q. Due north?

A. (*dryly, with a half smile*) No . . . not due north. . . . One would have been buried at sea . . . if that were the case. [He seemed to think that the cemetery was "bearing a bit eastward."]

Q. Was there a church nearby?

A. No . . . there was a church . . . in Calais.

Q. There was no church in the cemetery?

A. No.

Q. John, why did some of the Booths drop the "h" from the name and spell it, B-o-o t?

A. My name was Booth!

Q. I know that your name was Booth, but why did some drop the "h"?

A. Gervais' whole family did.

Q. Why?

A. Because . . . the French . . . could not pronounce "th."

Q. The French said, "Boot?"

A. Yes.

Q. John, was there a landmark near the cemetery?

A. A building . . . perhaps . . . three stories. There were the gates . . . into town. . . . Let's see . . . Where were the gates? . . . There were gates to the cemetery . . . and there were gates to the park . . . that had an arch above them . . . iron. . . . You passed through . . . the park . . . to go to the cemetery.

Q. You passed *through* the park to go to the cemetery?

A. By . . . by . . . beside or alongside.

Q. Was this park in Calais?

A. Yes . . . of course . . . there was a park in Calais . . . a large park. . . . I often met Marie there.

Q. What was the name of the road north of Calais the road leading to the park and the cemetery?

A. It was the main road . . . north of town.

Q. Were there other Booths buried in the cemetery?

A. Yes . . . Georges was buried there . . . my son.

It was with great difficulty that I managed to conceal my surprise—*if John were dead how could he know that Marie had born him a son?* While I was wondering how to frame my next question, Wesley's body stiffened suddenly, and he cried out, "Who is speaking?" It was the Booth voice tinged with hysteria. I tried to soothe him, but he became increasingly agitated. He started to thrash about and cried again, "It was a woman's voice, now what did she say?" This outburst was followed by some rapid words in French, which I could not understand. I became alarmed and told him that his memories were fading, but before orienting him again into his own life, suggested that on the following morning he would be able to drive directly to the gravesite.

Wesley remembered nothing of this regression, and the next morning after breakfast we headed out of town in a northerly direction. Reminders of war were all around us—fragments of bombed buildings and deep scars gouged in the earth by explosives.

We had driven about four miles when Wesley said simply, "We're close," and suddenly turned into a small lane that ended abruptly within a few feet. Our further passage was barred by a fence posted by the French Military. Although we could not read the signs, we knew that they meant "Keep Out!" We had no choice but to turn around. Wesley was sullen and silent as we headed back the way we had come. We had gone only a short distance when once again he slowed to make a turn. This time, the road we had turned into narrowed, becoming no more than a path choked with weeds, leading to an old churchyard.

There was no date on the church and it was locked, but we peered in through the windows and concluded that it had been in recent use. We noticed that the ground was hollowed out in many places as if graves had been opened and their contents removed—but long ago. I mentioned this to Wesley and he replied vaguely, "There was no church."

We agreed to look once more in the cemetery where we had begun our search, and drove there; but when we arrived, we couldn't find the caretaker, and wandered around by ourselves looking at names. The ground was covered with deep sand—we had difficulty walking, and before long became separated from each other. I found Wesley very quickly, but Lenny was nowhere to be seen. We didn't think it would be proper to shout in the cemetery, so Wesley and I started back toward the caretaker's cottage, because we were fairly certain that Lenny would have to head in that direction.

While walking along, a man suddenly appeared in front of us and asked, "English?" We nodded and he motioned us to follow him. I thought that perhaps he wanted to ask Wesley for money and I lagged behind, feeling uneasy about not finding Lenny. The cemetery was lonely and deserted and I began to fear that something might have happened to him.

When I spotted my husband coming toward me through the rows of gravestones, I was relieved, and quickly told him what had happened. We hurried to catch up with Wesley who was talking to another man who turned out to be a willing interpreter. The man who had spoken to us a moment before had vanished.

The caretaker pointed out a large and very old marker with the names, "Boot-Smith" engraved at the top. "No," I said, and explained that we were looking for James, Georges, or Gervais. By this time the caretaker's wife had joined us with two or three companions. In reply to a question from the man who translated for us, she said that the Booths we looked for, James and Georges, had been reburied in the "'Boot-Smith" grave. A 1905 law required that all burials be in municipal cemeteries, prohibiting burials in private ground.

We looked at the gravestones of the other Booths, hoping to find clues or a connection to Gervais Booth and his family, but we found nothing.

Wesley walked around the small area of English graves and stood still before a large marble monument bearing the clean, carved name, "Stubbs." Half aloud, Wesley remarked sadly, "I knew that man. . . ." If our interpreter thought that this was odd, he gave no sign,

174

but snapped his head toward the stone which bore the departure date, 1880. Stubbs, he said, had been a rich lace manufacturer from Nottingham, England. I did not think that Wesley had heard him; he appeared to be preoccupied with his own thoughts.

Meanwhile, I found a gravestone with the name "Eagle" inscribed on it: family of Eagle—Roper. If these were the parents of Booth's wife, the marking on the stone was strange indeed:

FAMILIE OF EAGLE—ROPER
In loving memory of William Frederick Eagle, 1807–1905
Of Martha Roper, his wife 1812–1905
Of Charles Eagle, son of the above, 1847–1907
Of Sarah Ann, daughter of the above, 1848–1928
Of Mary Eagle, 1854–1937

The name and age would make it possible for Mary Eagle to have been the wife of James Booth, but if so, why would she be listed as "Eagle," or if she was "Mary Eagle," why is "daughter of the above" not included after her name? I remembered that Booth had said many months ago, "They never considered us married." I thought at the time that he was referring to the townspeople, but could he have meant her parents? After his death had she taken back her family name? I had no answer to these questions, nor to the mysterious absence of the Gervais Booth family graves.

We returned to the town hall where the clerks, careful to keep their huge record books out of our sight, searched for Booths. They chattered among themselves and finally sent for a man who spoke English. He told us that no records were available and they could not help us further; but he added that the graves we looked for might possibly be under the old theatre building which was put up over a graveyard. When we asked what year it was built, he replied that he did not know, but that there was a "Boot" still in the lace manufacturing business in Calais. Our hopes rose again, and we went to meet him.

He was a very old man and we had difficulty understanding his English. He told us that his uncle had come to Calais in 1920—to start a lace factory. He did not know of a Gervais Booth; had never heard of an actor by the name of Booth, and did not think he was related. We thanked him and left, admitting to ourselves, finally, that our search seemed to have led us to a dead end.

On the morning of our departure from Calais, the sun was shining, but Wesley seemed very depressed. He sat inside the cabin of the ferry, not wanting to stand on deck to watch the receding shoreline. He was remote, and his eyes were no longer the eyes of Wesley. Instead, they were the brooding, tormented eyes of Booth. When I reached out to console him, he fell, sobbing, into my arms.

"I can't be . . . leaving," he cried, brokenly. "I know that I cannot leave Calais!" His words chilled me. His pronounciation of "Calais" had carried the soft, caressing sound that only Booth can give it. I felt an indescribable fear, mingled with relief, as the shoreline of Calais faded at last and disappeared. Wesley returned to us slowly, as the presence of Booth retreated into the dark recesses of his mind. He had closed the door to the past and buried the mystery in a solitary grave marked only in his memory—John Wilkes Booth.

Before we returned home, we visited Madame Tussaud's Wax Works in London. There, immortalized in wax in the Chamber of Horrors, are murderers and villains from every age, including Lee Harvey Oswald, assassin of President John F. Kennedy. There is no model of John Wilkes Booth. When I asked why, I was told that there never had been a model of John Wilkes Booth.

25
SOME FINAL THOUGHTS

THE JOHN WILKES BOOTH STORY MAY PROVE INTERESTING
to you the reader, but to me, it was far more than that. I
became his friend, and although he did not know who I
was, there seemed an intangible bond between us. Over
the many months of work he became a very real person,
and when the work was completed I suffered a deep
sense of loss, as though someone very special had passed
out of my life and was forever gone.

What has been proven by the Booth case? Some will
say "nothing" and others will claim it to be a real case for
reincarnation, for certainly there is much proof that
Booth's strange story is true. Arthur Sheehan and I have
many records and documents further substantiating
Booth's story, so many, in fact, that is was impossible to
include all of our findings into the book. The trails, clouded by time, were difficult to trace as they continually
crossed into broader areas until such a complicated

maze developed that I was unable to cope with it, much less, to distill it down for the reader.

Aside from all of the proof, the question remains, how did Booth break through? Was it reincarnation or was it an entity who claimed Wesley's body during hypnotic trance? In my own mind I have ruled out the "entity" possibility but then, I am a believer in reincarnation, so, no matter what I say, or how objective I think I am, truth always boils down to each individual accepting it as he sees it. Life in itself is a mystery, but the greater mystery is death, and down through the countless ages man has tried to cross that bridge to prove the eternity of his own existence. A searcher must weigh all of the evidence and try not to close the mind with the word, "Impossible."

What is impossible? Merely something that has not, as yet, become commonplace. Flying was once thought to be impossible. The invention of the light bulb, impossible, and just a few short years ago, it was thought an impossibility to set a man on the moon.

As the old Chinese proverb has it, "A long journey must begin with a single step." I feel that the Booth case has been another small step on the long journey toward a greater understanding concerning the many dimensions of man's wonderfully complex creation.

I am deeply indebted to Devin Garrity, my publisher, for his support in such a highly controversial work.

I should like to hear from you, the reader; I would be interested in learning your opinion of the case, and of any additional material that might add or detract from it.

The story of John Wilkes Booth was not of my own creation—I was merely the instrument that recorded the happenings and set them forth as honestly as I was able. I might also say that, many times during conversations with Booth, words seemed to flow through me from an unknown source, framing the questions that I asked. Arthur Sheehan and I have, at times, felt "guided" in the work by an unseen force.

I would like to close with the words of a mind reader called "Dunninger," who had a television program some years ago. He always ended his show with a few words that now seem most appropriate as an ending to my book: "To those who believe, no explanation is necessary. To those who do not believe, no explanation is possible."

BIBLIOGRAPHY

BOOKS

Bishop, Jim, *The Day Lincoln Was Shot*. Harper & Row, New York, 1955.

Carter, Samuel H., III, *The Riddle of Doctor Mudd*. G. P. Putnam's Sons, New York, 1974.

Clarke, Asia Booth, *The Unlocked Book, A Memoir of John Wilkes Booth by his sister Asia Booth Clarke*. G. P. Putnam's Sons, New York, 1938.

DeWitt, David M., *The Assassination of President Lincoln and Its Expiation.* Macmillan Co., New York, 1909.

Eisenschiml, Otto, *Why Was Lincoln Murdered?* Little, Brown and Co., Boston, 1937.

Forrester, Izola. *This One Mad Act*. Hale, Cushman & Flint, Boston, 1937.

Fowler, Robert H. "Did Stanton Plan Lincoln's Murder?" *Civil War Times*, Vol. III, No. 5, Aug., 1961.

Kimmel, Stanley, *The Mad Booths of Maryland*. Bobbs-Merrill Co., New York, 1940. Dover reprint, 1969.

Kunhardt and Kunhardt (Dorothy Meserve and Philip B. Jr.), *Twenty Days*. Harper & Row, New York, 1965.

Lockridge, Richard, *Darling of Misfortune*. The Century Co., New York-London, 1932.

Ruggles, Eleanor, *Prince of Players*. W. W. Norton & Co., New York, 1953.

PERIODICALS

Bridges, C.A., "The Knights of the Golden Circle: a Filibustering Fantasy." *Southwestern Historical Quarterly*, Vol. XLIV, No. 3, January, 1941.

Crenshaw, Ollinger, "The Knights of the Golden Circle: The Career of George Bickley." *American Historical Review*, Vol. XLVII.